Here's what experts are saying about
The Publishing Game:

**The Publishing Game:
Publish a Book in 30 Days**

"These 30-day books by Fern Reiss offer a viable way for
people to complete what may appear at first glance to be an
overwhelming job, one few people would otherwise tackle.
By breaking down time-consuming complicated processes
into simpler discrete steps that can be completed in a day,
**Reiss has opened up the world of writing and
publishing** books to people who have full-time jobs or other
responsibilities that give them little free time. So, even people
who work full time can publish a book in 30 days—although
they might take 30 Saturdays to do it. Just think: If you write
just one page a day, you can have a book in less than six
months! What are you waiting for?"—John Kremer,
1001 Ways to Market Your Book

The Publishing Game: Bestseller in 30 Days

"**Strategies designed to make the day job superfluous.**"
—Publishers Weekly

"*The Publishing Game* provides a day-by-day book promotion outline that will accurately lead you every step of the way. Now you can be assured that you are doing every possible thing to promote your book and you are doing it in the right order. **This book IS your marketing plan.**"—Dan Poynter, *The Self-Publishing Manual*

"**I wish more publishers would not only follow her step-by-step lesson plan but read this book BEFORE they start rolling the publishing dice.**"—Jan Nathan, Executive Director, Publishers Marketing Association

"**A very useful step-by-step overview of the daunting task of getting published.**"—Carl Lennertz, BookSense, American Booksellers Association

"**Positively awesome! Every writer should buy this book.**"—Rick Frishman, *Guerrilla Marketing for Writers*

"A step-by-step, day-by-day roadmap from complete unknown to bestseller. Packed with excellent resources. Follow every step and your chances of hitting the big-time go dramatically skyward. **Keep this book in the 'use it all the time' section of your bookshelf.**"—Shel Horowitz, *Grassroots Marketing: Getting Noticed in a Noisy World*

"**Packed with tips, tricks, names and websites,** this day-by-day plan will have you on your way to winning the publishing game before you even know it." —Mary Westheimer, www.BookZone.com, the Net's largest publishing community

"**A wealth of targeted instruction on how to drive your book to success.** I especially like the bullet point presentation method; it makes action steps easy to follow and fast to review. This book is a useful addition to the literature on the subject."—Marilyn Ross, *Jump Start Your Book Sales*

"**A superbly presented, day-by-day, user-friendly guide** written by experienced publisher Fern Reiss for the purpose of aiding the novice publisher in applying a series of promotional and marketing techniques ranging from being featured in national magazines, to non-bookstore sales venues, to the role and uses of publishing industry awards, to print/broadcast publicity campaigns, to author speaking tours, to self-syndication, to the utilization of email newsletters and more, which would aptly service to increase sales of self-published and small-press published titles. A solid, practical guide offering tips, tricks and techniques as well as a useful structure by which to undertake the tactics that most other how-to books on publishing offer in only broad, general terms rather than specific daily activities. Informed and informative, The Publishing Game is very highly recommended as an essential basic reading, especially for those new to the field of publishing."—James Cox, Midwest Book Review

"**A significant addition to the self-publisher's library, offering both in-depth coverage and a unique, calendar-based sequence.**"—John Culleton, Rowse Reviews

"A great guerilla marketing plan. Writers, you absolutely need this book."—Bob Spear, Heartland Reviews

"A powerful addition to the classics in the field."
—Pat Bell, *THE Prepublishing Handbook*

The Publishing Game:
Find an Agent in 30 Days

"Chock full of terrific, insider secrets—a must-read for any author seeking a top notch agent! And what writer isn't?"—Lisa Collier Cool, *How to Write Irresistible Query Letters* and former literary agent

"Brimming with publishing wisdom that will help you get the agent and publisher you want—fast."—Michael Larsen, Michael Larsen – Elizabeth Pomada Literary Agency

Other Books by Fern Reiss

The Publishing Game: Bestseller in 30 Days

The Publishing Game: Find an Agent in 30 Days

Kids Publish!

Consultants Publish

Expertizing

Terrorism and Kids: Comforting Your Child

The Infertility Diet: Get Pregnant and
Prevent Miscarriage

Other Offerings from
Peanut Butter and Jelly Press

Literary Agents Kit

Sell Your Books to Corporations Kit

Top Amazon Reviewers Kit

Independent Bookstores Publicity Kit

Email Newsletter Kit

Syndicate Yourself Kit

Special Reports Kit

The Publishing Game:
Publish a Book in 30 Days

by Fern Reiss

Peanut Butter and Jelly Press
Boston, Massachusetts

To receive a **free hot contacts sheet** with names, info, and emails for top magazine editors, talk show hosts, reviewers, and more, email PubNewsletter@PublishingGame.com or register at our website, www.PublishingGame.com.

Attention corporations, writing organizations and writing conferences: Take 40% off and use our books as fundraisers, premiums, or gifts. Please contact the publisher:

Peanut Butter and Jelly Press, LLC
P.O. Box 590239
Newton, Massachusetts 02459-0002
(617)630-0945
info@PublishingGame.com
www.PBJPress.com
SAN 299-7444

Library of Congress Cataloging-in-Publication Data

Reiss, Fern.
  The publishing game. Publish a book in 30 days / by Fern Reiss.
     p. cm.
  Includes bibliographical references and index.
  ISBN 1-893290-85-9
1. Self publishing—United States. I. Title.
Z285.5 .R45 2003
070.5'93—dc21   2002151551

10 9 8 7 6 5 4 3 2 1

Cover by Mayapriya Long, Bookwrights.com

Dedication

Thanks to everyone who made this book possible—my family, particularly my husband Jonathan, for not only putting up with the pace but thriving on it, and my three wonderful kids, Benjamin, Daniel, and Ariel, who provide such wonderful ways to procrastinate.

Thanks again to Seattle's Best Coffee in Newton Center, definitely the best place in Boston to write books. Just seeing that Seattle's sign now triggers a Pavlovian urge to type. The reverse, unfortunately, is also true.

Most of all, this book is dedicated to you, the reader, who is thinking of starting out on the independent publishing adventure. Go for it! We are living in an exciting time for independent publishing. I hope you'll seize the opportunity to publish your own book, your own way. And I hope you'll enjoy it as much as I have.

Love to all,

Fern

Contents

Introduction 13
   So, you want to publish a book! 13
   In 30 days? 14
   Can self-publishing be successful? 15
   One last word before you begin...............................17
Week Number One 19
   Decide to Self-Publish 20
   Define Your Goals 22
   Zero-in on a Hot Subject 23
   Define Your Target Audience 27
   Choose a Title 29
   Write the Cover Copy 33
   Set the Book's Price 35
   Choose a Publication Date 41
   Write Your Business Plan..43
   Create Your Financial Plan 47
Week Number Two..55
   Choose Your Company Name 56
   Choose Financial Software 57
   Set Up Your Legal Structure 62
   Learn About the Legalities......................................66
   Establish Your Company 72
   Get an ISBN 75
   Fill Out an ABI..79
   Set a Discount Schedule and Terms.........................81
   Plan Your Future Titles 84
   Create Your Website 87
   Decide How to Sell Your Books...............................93
   Make a Progress Chart 127

Week Number Three...129
  Create a Support Network...130
  Order a Barcode...135
  Send for a Copyright Form 139
  Finalize Your Cover Copy 140
  Zero-in on a Cover Designer 142
  Plan Your Cover Art...144
Week Number Four...149
  Choose an Editor..150
  Finalize Your Manuscript...153
  Send Advance Galleys to Reviewers 155
  Send Advance Galleys to Chain Stores............................164
  Request Cataloging in Publication Data..........................168
Week Number Five...175
  Lay Out Your Book...176
  Plan Your Front Matter..185
  Plan Your Back Matter...190
  Locate Printers 194
  Submit RFQs to Printers 199
Week Number Six...209
  Do a Pre-Print Final Check..210
  Submit Your Book to the Printer 212
  Ship Your Books from the Printer 213
  List Your Book and Publishing House.............................216
  List Your Book With Online Bookstores.........................218
  Organize Your Shipping Department...............................220
  Organize for Returns..230
  Review and Renew Your Business and Financial Plans 232
  Plan for the Next Book...233
Appendix A: Bibliography...237
Appendix B: Budget..239
Index...245
About the Author 251

Introduction

Cʒ Ȣ

So, you want to publish a book!

The opportunity to publish exists as never before. Even as few as ten years ago, the only real option for authors was to bang their heads against the establishment wall, querying agents and publishers endlessly. Today, it is possible to publish your book yourself, easily—design a cover, secure a printer, enlist a wholesaler, get your book into bookstores and libraries. Anyone can do it. All you need is a plan. This book is that plan.

Now you can not only publish yourself, you can actually make money at it. There are over 50,000 independent publishers in America today, generating an estimated annual $14 billion in book sales. You can be one of them.

You can move faster than the big publishing houses. Most big publishers will sit on your manuscript for months, then send you a form rejection letter. Even if you could get a big publisher to accept your book—an increasingly difficult proposition—it would take them at least nine to 18 months to bring it to press. You can do it yourself in a matter of weeks.

You're in charge if you publish yourself. You can write your own book, choose your own cover. With a big publisher, you lose control of that process. They make all the decisions. If you publish yourself, you decide.

You can also keep your book on shelves longer if you're in the driver's seat. Most big publishers allow the bulk of their titles to disappear from bookstores in about eight months. But if you publish yourself, you can keep promoting your titles indefinitely, and keep those books where they belong— in bookstores!

You can sell fewer books than the big publishers do—and still make money. (If you publish your book traditionally, you'll get 10% royalty. That means for every $20 book your publisher sells, you'll make two bucks. If you publish yourself, you make the whole $20 (minus $2-3 dollars in printing and other costs) which means you don't need to sell nearly as many books as you would if you were an author selling through a large publishing house to make exactly the same amount!) Furthermore, books that are not cost-effective for the big publishing houses to undertake with sales of only 5,000 can still make you $100,000! You can make enough to give up your day job.

You just need to know how.

In 30 days?

That's where this book comes in. I'm going to take you, step by step, through the process of creating a book, from manuscript to published product. You won't learn much about marketing your book; if you want to learn how to take your book to bestseller status, read the sequel to this book, **The Publishing Game: Bestseller in 30 Days**. (A small amount of material—on creating a website, and submitting your book to reviewers—is covered in both books. And some of the introductory days' activities in this book overlap with those in **The Publishing Game: Find an Agent in 30 Days**, a book for authors trying to publish traditionally.) But in the next 30 days, you'll learn everything you need to know to create a published book. You'll find out how to organize your publishing house, meet the legal requirements, and plan a budget. You'll lay out your book, have it edited, design the book's cover, and find a printer. You'll figure out how to fulfill and ship orders, and how to manage your finances.

Most of all—you'll have a lot of fun.

You may not want to do everything suggested here. And you may want to work faster, or slower, and take more or less time than our suggested 30 days. But this book will give you a framework within which to organize your publishing tasks.

Just for the record, you *can* do it in the 30 days suggested here—I have. But for your first independent publishing experience, you might enjoy it more if you take more time and progress through the steps at a more leisurely pace.

Can self-publishing be successful?

That depends, of course, on what you mean by *successful*. But yes, it can definitely be successful. By independently publishing you can get a book into the market that would not otherwise have been printed. You can make money doing so. Moreover, though people may sniff because you didn't use a *real* publisher, there's a fine tradition of self-publishing in America. The following works were all originally self-published; some of them went on to sell to a larger publisher, and most of them brought fame, or fortune, or both, to their authors:

Familiar Quotations by John Bartlett
The One-Minute Manager by Blanchard and Johnson
What Color is Your Parachute? by Richard Bolles
Life's Little Instruction Book by Jackson Brown
Juggling for the Complete Klutz by John Cassidy
The Wealthy Barber by David Chilton
Your Erroneous Zones by Wayne Dyer
Science and Health by Mary Baker Eddy
The Christmas Box by Rick Evans
The Beanie Baby Handbook by Lee and Sue Fox
Poor Richard's Almanac by Benjamin Franklin
How to See Europe on $5 a Day by Arthur Frommer
A Time to Kill by John Grisham
Feed Me! I'm Yours! by Vicky Lansky
Lady Chatterly's Lover by D.H. Lawrence
Real Peace by Richard Nixon
In Search of Excellence by Tom Peters
The Celestine Prophecy by James Redfield
Robert's Rules of Order by Henry Robert
The Joy of Cooking by Irma Rombauer
The Encyclopedia of Associations by Fred Ruffner
The Jungle by Upton Sinclair
The Elements of Style by William Strunk
Walden by Henry Thoreau
Huckleberry Finn by Mark Twain
Leaves of Grass by Walt Whitman

The entry barriers to independent publishers are high. True, by independently publishing you bypass the agents and publishers who wouldn't even unwrap your manuscript. You have control.

Unfortunately, unless you have a direct line to your customers, you may nonetheless find it difficult to get your book into circulation. Wholesalers don't want to talk to single-book publishers; you won't be able to get library cataloging numbers easily; and most professional reviewers will toss aside your book in the same way the agents and publishers tossed your manuscript.

On the other hand, there are creative ways to bypass these entry barriers. This book tells you how.

One last word before you begin

Although we verify and update this information each and every time we reprint the book, the nature of the world (and certainly, the nature of the world wide web) is that information that's current today is obsolete tomorrow. Please continue to check the website `PublishingGame.com` for the latest additions, deletions, and changes to this volatile information. And please help us keep this information helpful to publishers! If you spot an inaccuracy, or try a website, an email address, or any service or vendor that's not satisfactory, please email us at `PubComments@Publishing Game.com` so that we can change it in the next printing. Thanks so much!

Finally, remember to enjoy the experience. Whether you're an author who is determined to have your book make a difference or a publisher who is tired of being told you can't, it *is* possible to publish your book yourself, make money at it, and enjoy the process. So have fun!

Week Number One

Cʒ ʓↄ

This week you'll:

- **Be sure you want to self publish**
- **Define your goals**
- **Zero-in on a hot subject**
- **Define your target audience**
- **Choose a title and subtitle for your book**
- **Write the cover copy**
- **Set the book's price**
- **Choose a publication date**
- **Create your financial plan**
- **Write your business plan**

Day Number 1

Today, you'll **consider whether you really want to self publish** and **define your goals**.

Decide to Self-Publish

Independent publishing, or publishing your own books, yourself, your way, can be a thrilling experience—or it can be a nightmare. Before you take the plunge, consider whether you are going into independent publishing for the right reasons—and whether your expectations are realistic:

- *You won't have to work as hard.* The reality is that self-publishing involves writing, editing, designing, marketing, and about a million other activities. Many small publishers have never worked this hard in the rest of their professional lives. (Of course, it's more fulfilling, too!)

- *You won't have a boss.* True: Instead you'll have dozens. They're called readers—and wholesalers, and distributors—and if you want your business to be successful, you will have to pay more attention to them than you've ever paid to your boss.

- *You can make piles of money.* While independent publishing can be quite profitable, the reality is that many independent publishers don't make a profit. Although the up-front expenses in publishing are small, poor product—or poor marketing—can doom your project to failure. So before you plan to quit your day job, be sure you have a plan for making your book—and business—succeed.

- *You can deduct all your expenses and pay no taxes.* Think again: IRS rules about home businesses have gotten tougher and tougher, and taxes take quite a bite out of that book income. (And unless you're showing a profit at least three out of every five years, the IRS considers your business a hobby—and as such, it isn't eligible for *any* deductions.)

- *You can do the interesting work, and skip the rest.* Only if you're planning to pay to have someone else do the boring bits. There are few independent publishers who are equally fascinated by all aspects of the job: Perhaps you like the writing, but not the marketing; perhaps you love the public relations, but hate packing those orders. While it is true that you can spare yourself the mundane tasks, you will have to pay someone else to do them.

If you're a self-disciplined self-starter, who makes decisions quickly and easily, likes to plan but also likes the fun of risk, enjoys challenges but knows there will be boring bits, who likes public speaking (not a requirement, but it certainly does make book promotion easier!) and is supported by a family and friends in starting your own publishing house, you are likely to enjoy publishing.

Define Your Goals

You can achieve your goals—but before you can achieve them, you need to define them. And most importantly, you need to write them down. Studies have shown that the act of writing down and quantifying your goals makes them more attainable. So here's what to think about:

- Why do you want to be a publisher?

- What type of book do you want to publish?

- What are you hoping to attain as a publisher? (Fame and prestige? Helping the people who need the information? Financial rewards? Media attention?)

- How many books do you want to publish in the next two years? Five years? Ten years?

- How much money do you want to make? How many books do you want to sell? Be specific!

Next, type up your list, and hang it over your desk so that you can see it while you work. (Reviewing concrete goals works for dieters and corporate strategists, so put it to work for you!)

Day Number 2

Today, you'll **zero-in on a hot subject** for your book, define your **target audience**, and **choose a title and subtitle** for your book.

Zero-in on a Hot Subject

This book assumes that you already have a polished manuscript in hand. Before you invest any more time in publishing it, you need to make sure it's the right book, and that it's a saleable book. Sometimes, even a slight shift of focus or slant is enough to transform a book from ho-hum to hot. To discover whether your book is appropriate and salcable in the marketplace, you need to do some market research. Here's how:

- First, make sure you want to write and speak about the topic you're considering for the next three to five years. If you're going to get bored promoting the subject earlier than that, choose a different topic.

- Make sure you can write a two or three-line bio for yourself that makes you sound like a credible person to be writing about the topic. "John likes ice skating a lot" probably doesn't cut it, though "John has been a semi-professional ice skater for 30 years and is Founder of *Ice International*" does.

- Certain topics are always hot. If your book is on weight loss, exercise, spirituality, or cooking, you've identified a potential best selling topic.

- If your book is aimed at a focused market that is extremely large (such as teenagers) or rapidly growing (such as seniors), it's a good bet that your book will sell well.

- Make sure your book is aimed at an audience that both reads and spends money on books. (A book meant to be read by illiterates, for example, probably won't sell.) It also doesn't do much good to write a book for an audience that does not buy books. Also, make sure your audience has the money to pay speakers if you're planning to leverage your writing and speaking—highly recommended!

- Be sure your topic is focused enough. A round-up book on cancer probably wouldn't have sold nearly as well as *The Cancer Diet*. Similarly, had the book you are reading been called *All About Publishing* it probably wouldn't have appealed as much to people specifically looking for information on how to self-publish. Focusing your book so it appeals to *some* people is almost always more effective than trying to make it appeal to *everyone*.

- Make sure the slant is saleable and easily marketable. Choose a subject that is: new or hasn't been done before; that you can mold into sounding new by adding some new material; that incorporates money or sex (both of which always sell); that promises the reader tremendous benefits; that goes against the accepted wisdom; or that is humorous, startling, or otherwise attention-grabbing.

- Check out your subject on Amazon.com, or one of the other online booksellers. See how many books they already have on the topic, and how your book is different. (Copy down the ISBN numbers—Amazon calls them ASIN numbers and they're usually in tiny print under the graphic of the book cover—of any books that are similar.) See how highly they're ranked on Amazon (check both their popularity number, and how quickly Amazon will ship them—if they're in enough demand, Amazon will usually say, "Ships in 24 hours.")

- Next, go to the bookstore. Consider where exactly your book would be put in the bookstore. Make sure that is the genre in which you want to be placed. Look to see how much shelf space that topic gets. If there are hundreds of books on your topic, the market may already be saturated, unless your slant is different. On the other hand, if you only spot one or two titles, it's hard to know whether you've chosen a topic that is unpopular, or whether you've identified something that will soon take off. If you can, strike up a relationship with the bookstore owner, and get some advice. Ask how well competing titles are selling. Before you go home, compile a list of titles similar to yours and their ISBN numbers (that's the ten-digit number on the barcode of the book, usually preceded by the letters ISBN, which stands for International Standard Book Number.)

- Next, call the sales line for Ingram, the largest book wholesaler in the country, and find out how well they have done with similar titles. Call the recorded message at (615)213-6803 and be prepared to key in the ISBN numbers of competitive titles that you found at the bookstore and on Amazon. Are books on your topic selling well?

- Next, take your idea to your local library. Befriend a librarian, ideally in the part of the library where your book will be placed (if it's a children's book, get to know a children's librarian; if a reference book, talk to a reference librarian.) Introduce yourself, and explain you're thinking about writing a book. Ask your librarian if there's a need for it. Find out if there's a way to tweak your book to make it more appealing for the library market. (Before you leave, ask if your friendly librarian would mind taking a look at it once it's done. If you're unable to get a review from one of the major library journals, the next best thing would be an endorsement from your local librarian—librarians tend to trust other librarians!)

- Do some informal surveys. Ask book-loving friends whether they see a need for your book, and whether they would buy it. Friends won't want to hurt your feelings, but if you give them a choice of slant—"My next book is either going to be *Day Dreams of Dogs* or *Encouraging Spirituality in Your Pet*, which do you prefer?" they may be more comfortable giving you an honest answer.

- Finally, check out other publishers' catalogs (you can write them directly and just ask for them.) Check out publishers' stands at book fairs and tradeshows.

Define Your Target Audience

The most important step in devising a market strategy for your book is determining who your target audience is, and how you can reach them.

- Here are some questions to consider in trying to zero-in on your elusive audience, and how your book relates to them:

    o Who is a typical reader of your book? (Be certain your typical reader likes to *read* and spends money on books!)

    o Where does he live? Where does he work? How old is he?

    o How much money does he make? What does he spend his discretionary money on?

    o What organizations does he belong to? (Be certain these organizations can afford to pay you to speak on your topic.)

    o Where does he spend his free time?

    o Where does he hang out online?

    o Where does he buy his books?

    o How many people are there like him? *How big is your audience?*

    o Why does he need your book? What problem does he have that it will solve?

- o Does he need the book enough to pay the price? And what price will he pay?

- o Does any other book on the market currently serve his needs? If so, how is your book different?

- o What are his book buying needs now? What books will he need in the future?

- Now that you have thought a little more about who your audience is, begin thinking about how you can reach it. Don't just say, "My book will be in bookstores, and that's how people will find it." If you can't rattle off at least ten great ways to get your book into the hands of your potential audience, you're not yet ready to publish it. Consider the following:

  - o What recreational activities does your audience engage in which would be possible venues for selling your book?

  - o What professional associations might consider quantity sales of your title for their members?

  - o What other products do your potential readers purchase, and how can you link your book to those products?

  - o What websites do your prospects shop and browse? How can you publicize or sell your book on those sites?

  - o What magazines, newspapers, and newsletters does your audience read? What sorts of editorial content could you contribute to such publications?

o   What online mailing lists and discussion groups does your audience read? Are you already an active participant in those forums?

- Now, make an action list of at least 25 things you can do, *starting today,* to find your prospects and discuss your book with them, in locations that aren't bookstores. Include organizations to join or in which to get more involved, webmasters to write, alternative retail outlets to explore. Now write one item on your calendar for each of the next five weeks—or add them directly to the day's tasks in this book—and spend a few minutes *every day* exploring these prospects. It's never too early to start marketing your book. (For more marketing strategies, see the companion book, **The Publishing Game: Bestseller in 30 Days**.)

Choose a Title

For some people, choosing the title (and subtitle) are the hardest parts of writing a book. Here are some things to consider in choosing a title:

- Be sure the title conveys what the book is about. The example everyone uses for this rule is *What Color is Your Parachute* which is, of course, not about parachutes but career counseling. Although this book broke the rule and got away with it, picking an appropriate title will help you more effectively sell your book to readers, because they will more easily be able to find it.

- The title should be concise and catchy; the subtitle should somehow expand on or explain the title, or for whom the book is intended.

- If possible put the most important "keyword" as the first word in the title. Instead of calling it, "Tricks You Can Teach Dogs," try "Dogs and Tricks". That way, when people do a search for "dogs," your book pops up first.

- Try to pick a title that tells the point of the book, in as few words as possible.

- Consider that for certain books, humorous titles sell better than serious titles.

- Try to zero-in on a title that will *compel* people to pluck the book off a bookshelf. Twists on standard expressions work particularly well (as in the bestselling *Tongue Fu!*)

- In the title, sell the book's benefits (Lose weight fast!) not features (an eating plan). Sell the answer (Make money by selling goldfish!) not the question (How can you save enough for retirement?)

- Emphasize the book's value to the reader in monetary savings (Make Money!), time savings (In 30 Days!), or desired change of life (Retire! Have More Fun! Eat More, Lose More!)

- Try to make the title exclusive (The Confidential Guide to…) rather than generic (The Common Guide to…)

- Choose a title that can also double as a workshop title, a website name, a radio show… You get the idea.

- Choose a title that would work for a series as well as a single book; if the book is successful, you have the option to keep going with it, and build on the publicity, name-recognition, and readers you already have.

- Keep the main title short and punchy. Use the subtitle to explain the details if necessary.

- Make sure you check in the directory, *Books in Print* and online—this is a great use for Amazon.com—to see if anyone else is using your book title before you finalize it. Run the title through several internet search engines as well, to make sure no one else is using it. You can't copyright a title—so legally, unless the title is also trademarked, it's not a problem if more than one book has the same title. But it's not recommended; you want readers to be able to find *you*, not the other book.

- Ask professional acquaintances to help you narrow your list down to the top five or six choices.

- Check to see whether the website domain names are available for your top choices. (Do this by going to www.Verisign.com and checking availability.) If you can lock in the domain name for your book title (which will also be the same as your presentation title for talks and workshops) it makes it much easier for customers, workshop organizers, Amazon buyers, and the media to find you. (Check out InfertilityDiet.com, TerrorismAndKids.com, and PublishingGame.com.)

- Next, excerpt part of your book into an article. (Not the whole book—just a representative section.) Then offer the article—with different titles—to industry magazines and related Internet sites. See which titles seem to elicit the most interest and response. The best title for the book is the one in which the most people seem to be interested.

- Keep in mind that Amazon and other search engines list numbers before letters. So "100 Tips on Publishing" would be listed before "Hundreds of Tips on Publishing." Consider starting your title with a number if appropriate.

- Bring your three top choices to a few local bookstores and libraries, and get some professional advice. Booksellers and librarians can often point out pluses or minuses in titles that you may have overlooked.

- Before you finalize your choice, practice saying the title a few times. You want your title to roll trippingly off the tongue. Make sure you can say it quickly and easily. If you can't say it easily now, in the comfort and privacy of your living room, it's a sure bet that it will get stuck coming out when you're promoting it on a radio show or in a workshop.

- If you're going to write a series of books, you might want to consider trademarking the title of the series. (It's probably not worthwhile to do this for one book, even though your title can't be copyrighted.) You can find out more information on trademarks from the federal Patent and Trademark office, Commissioner for Trademarks, 2900 Crystal Drive, Arlington, VA 22202-3513, (800)786-9199, www.USPTO.gov.

Day Number 3

Today you'll write the **cover copy** for your book, set the **book's price**, and choose a **publication date**.

Write the Cover Copy

It may seem counter-intuitive to write the cover text for your book now. After all, you don't need the cover for a while, and aren't there more important things to do first?

In truth, writing the text for the cover is one of the most important tasks you'll do, and one you should seriously consider contracting out to a professional. The cover copy will sell—or not sell—your book. It is probably the second ingredient—the first would be the actual design of the front cover—in determining whether someone will decide to purchase your book. Although everyone—reviewers, booksellers, librarians—will tell you that it's what's *inside* your book that matters, the truth is that exceptional cover copy may be able to sell even a mediocre book, while ho-hum cover copy will blunt enthusiasm for even a magnificent book.

So make sure your cover text is superlative. Here's how:

- Do it yourself.

    o Think about your book—and why people will buy it.

o Then, instead of writing down *features* of the book, write the *benefits* to the reader. (A feature of **The Publishing Game: Find an Agent in 30 Days** is a listing of agents. But one *benefit* to readers is that they can easily locate an appropriate agent for their book. See the difference?)

o Pick out the three to five most important benefits— and make a bulleted list out of them. (List the items that you, as a reader, would get most excited about.)

o At the very top of the cover, over the list, write a killer one-liner that will make *everyone* in your target market pick up and leaf through the book. Don't just repeat the title. And make it as provocative as possible.

o Make up your ideal endorsement or two, preferably from people who are famous or important in the same, or a closely related, field. You may want to write to them now to ask for their advice; if you've written to them to ask for their advice, you are more likely to get a quotation when you request it.

o Add a few brief lines of punchy description.

o Don't overcrowd your cover with too much prose— people want to skim it quickly. The most successful covers (in terms of book sales) have a lot of white space that is text-free. Cover experts advise using 10 to 15 words on the front cover, and 75-200 words on the back cover. Don't be tempted to overwrite: Less is definitely more.

o   End with a sales pitch. All good salespeople know that it's not enough to intrigue—before you leave the client, you need to bring in the sale. So at the bottom of your cover text, put in a line that will encourage browsers to buy your book.

• Hire someone. If you're perfectly content to write your book, but find it very difficult to write punchy cover copy, you're not alone. Unless you can do superb cover copy, consider hiring someone who can. If you're going to hire someone to write your cover copy, make sure you choose someone who has experience in writing copy for *book covers*. There's an art to writing cover copy, and while there are many good editors and copy writers in the world, not all of them are trained in writing book cover copy. Here are a few excellent cover copy writers:

o   Shel Horowitz, Accurate Writing and More, PO Box 1164, Northampton, MA   01061, (413)586-2388, Shel@FrugalFun.com

o   Martha M. Bullen, Compelling Cover Copy, 125 South Valley Road, Paoli, PA   19301, (610)695-9919, WriterMB@aol.com

Set the Book's Price

Pricing is one of the most complicated steps in producing a book. Setting the wrong price will affect your sales on both the micro level (bookstore browsers will discard your book in favor of a more appropriately-priced book) and on the macro level (chain store buyers and distributors will be reluctant to carry the book if it's mispriced.) Price the book too high and people will be put off; price it too low, and people may think its quality inferior. Determining the "right" price is an art, not a science, and there are three basic methods publishers use to do their pricing.

- The first method involves pricing your book so you can make money on it. This is the formula most independent publishers are told to follow:

  o Start with the base production cost of your book— how much it will cost you to print them, in the quantity you're printing. Let's assume, for this example, that it will cost you $2 per book to print.

  o Multiply that production cost by eight. For our sample book, that brings the retail cost up to $16 per book.

  o Now we're going to work backwards, to show you what happens to that $16 price, which sounds like a fair bit of money. First, wholesalers will take 55% of that $16, leaving you with a net of $7.20. If you're working with a distributor, you will lose an additional 25% of that, leaving you with $5.40. The production cost of that book was, you'll remember, $2 per book, so subtract that, leaving you with a grand total of $3.40. Subtract the fee you owe the cover artist— figure an estimated $1000 cover price, amortized over a 3,000 book print run; that's roughly $0.33 per book, down to $3.07. Don't forget that you also have overhead—rent, utilities, etc—as well as publicity, advertising, postage, and such, bringing the total net down to, let's assume, $2.67 per book.

That figure gives you only $ .40 per book for those costs—which, assuming a 3,000 book print run, is only $1,200 total; many publishers spend a great deal more.) Then there's the cost of doing business with bookstores—figure another half dollar per book lost in returns, money tied up in inventory, storage costs, etc. That brings your total down to only about $2.17 per book in profit! (That means your 3,000 book print run—assuming you sell all those books—will generate exactly $6,510 in profit. Not exactly a get-rich-quick scheme.) Note: If you print more than 3,000 copies, or go back to re-print, you'll have to alter these numbers to eliminate the cover art price, which you'll already have paid for. Even so, you'll only end up with $2.47 in profit on subsequent books.

- The second method—which is the one I recommend, despite the fact that it means your already slim profits might be cut even slimmer—involves pricing your book so that *people will buy it*. My reasoning is simple: You might determine the "fair" price using the first method, but if no one wants to buy your book, what good does it do you?

  o Go to a bookstore. Look at all the books that are similar to yours. (I know, I know—there aren't any that are like yours—that's why you're publishing in the first place. But there have to be some books that are in some way similar. Find the closest approximations.)

  o Compare your book's physical characteristics. If all the similar books are hardcover, and yours is softcover, you can't charge as much (and vice versa). If all the others are 300 pages, and yours is 150 pages, the same is true.

o   Based on the similar books—and accounting for the physical differences (which are easier to gauge than the qualitative differences), work up a base price that seems in line with the competition.

o   Do not neglect this step! When you think you have a fair price, bring your book to the owner or manager of one or more bookstores. Show them whatever you have—and if you don't have anything yet, tell them what you are planning, and how it compares (physically) to the competition. Ask them what they would consider a fair retail price for your book. And then approximate that price as closely as possible. Most booksellers know their price points far better than we publishers ever will. Trust them.

o   Then, when you've set a bookstore-approved price, go back to the number analysis above, and plug in your new price. Make sure, before you embark on this experience, that you will actually be able to make a profit—however small—on every book you sell. (And remember that traditional pricing wisdom suggests that people are more likely to purchase if the item costs $1.95 than $2.00.)

•   The third method of pricing involves zeroing in on the price point that will yield the greatest total revenue in sales (which will not always be the highest per-book price.)

o First, calculate the number of possible buyers. If you have a book on how to de-clutter your home, and 100,000 Americans want to de-clutter their houses, then 100,000 is your total possible universe of buyers.

o But of course, no book will ever sell to all its potential buyers: Some of the potential buyers won't be as interested in the topic, some won't learn of the book's existence, etc. Traditional publishing wisdom suggests that at the *lowest* price point and most attractive sales terms, no more than 10% of all potential buyers will purchase. So at best, 10,000 people (10% of the total possible 100,000) will want to purchase your book. That is your largest possible audience.

o Remember, that 10,000 figure only applies at the most attractive terms—that is, the lowest book price. So, using your lowest possible book price (once you've factored in manufacturing and other costs), calculate how much revenue this audience will generate if they all (10,000 of them) purchase the book at the lowest (cheapest) price point. In other words, if your manufacturing and other costs are low enough that you could realistically sell the book for $5 each, then your total revenue generated would be $50,000 (10,000 people multiplied by $5).

o At higher price points, of course, fewer people in that universe of 100,000 will purchase: If the book costs $10 or $15, fewer potential purchasers will become actual buyers. So now, calculate how many people will buy at each of a few more higher prices. For example, if 10% of the total audience will buy at $5, perhaps only 6% will buy at $10 and only 2% at $15. So your total revenue at a $10 sales price is $60,000 (6% of 100,000 people is 6,000; if each buys a $10 book that generates $60,000); your total revenue at a $20 sales price is $30,000 (2% of 100,000 people is 2,000; if each buys a $15 book that generates $30,000.)

o Compare your total projected revenue figures. At $5 per book, your total revenue would be $50,000; at $10 per book $60,000, and at $15 per book, $30,000. This means that you should set your price at $10, which will generate the largest revenue ($60,000). This may seem counter-intuitive—you might think you would make the most money at the lowest price, since you will maximize how many people buy—but at the lower price, your total revenues are decreased despite having more buyers.

o One caveat: There is no way to know, precisely, what percentage of people in your target audience will purchase, and all the numbers in these examples are predicated upon guessing those crucial percentages. (If the percentages are wrong, then so are the projected revenues.) However, publishing wisdom suggests that not more than 10% of potential buyers will purchase at *any* price, and of course the percentage that will purchase decreases as the price increases. So although the precise numbers may be inaccurate, the *trend* will be accurate—and the wisdom that neither the highest, nor the lowest, price generally yields the most revenue.

You also need to choose your book's price carefully because it's tedious, time-consuming, and expensive to change it down the road. To change it, you have to sticker the new price on all of your books in stock, obtain a new barcode and reprint your books, and change the information in a variety of databases like Bowker's ISBN database.

Choose a Publication Date

Publication dates are arbitrary creations. Here's how to set yours:

- Your book's publication date has nothing to do with its print date (the day it comes back from the printer), and indeed, should be several months later.

- Reviewers insist on seeing advance galleys of the book, and seeing them at least *three to six months* before official publication date. (So if you are sending galleys to reviewers in January, better have a publication date of June or beyond.)

- Remember that buyers will need to see the books long before the official publication/release date, so that the books can be in bookstores by the pub date. (So, for example, if you want your book in stores in time for Christmas—don't we all?—you need to get it to the buyers at least six months before that.)

- Publishing wisdom suggests that it is best to avoid a publication date in the fall (because you're competing with the largest publishers' Christmas releases) and the spring (the second busiest time.) A mid-winter or summer publication date generally fares best.

- Holiday books should, obviously, be keyed for publication at least several months before the holiday.

- "Seasonal" books do best in the appropriate season. (Set a winter publication date for books on woodstoves or skiing; set a summer publication date for books on the beach.) With advance purchases, your book will end up on the shelves in time for its publication date, timed for the appropriate season.

Day Number 4

Today, you'll **begin writing a business plan** for your publishing house.

Write Your Business Plan

A business plan is an overall plan for the development of your book and publishing house. Entrepreneurs have all sorts of reasons for why they avoid writing business plans: It will take too long. It's too complex for what's really a simple business. You don't need a formal plan if you're the only person in the business. You don't have all the information you need to write a business plan. You're not applying for a bank loan, so you don't need to do this step. And so forth.

And though books on publishing abound, none offers the new publisher a business plan.

Yet, to achieve goals, you need a plan. If you're going to compete in a marathon, you make up a training schedule. If you're going to apply to graduate schools, you make up a list of requirements. If you want to lose weight, you find a diet and (try to) follow it. It's virtually impossible to succeed without a plan.

If you want to create a business, first you need to create a business plan. Otherwise, you will never have more than a hobby.

A business plan will organize your thinking and sort out your priorities. It will keep you on track. It will prevent you from reacting to emergencies, rather than sticking to your goals. It will keep your business on track not just this year, but in the years to come. It will help you succeed as a publisher.

Here's how to write a business plan for your publishing house:

- Start with a statement of purpose. Just write: "My publishing goal is_____." If you're planning to create recipe books for various medical conditions, for example, you could write, "To provide quick and easy menu plans and recipes for sufferers of infertility, diabetes, and heart disease." Include both the type of books you're planning (recipe books) and the type of audience you're writing for (sufferers of various medical conditions.) This simple exercise will also give you the infamous "elevator line," which you'll need later when you want to describe your business to others: The rule of thumb is, you should be able to explain it to a complete stranger in the course of a 30-second elevator ride.

- Describe the publishing house: Include its location, type of books you will publish, future directions you may move in, and qualities that make your publishing house special.

- Describe your market.

  o Who is your audience?

  o How large is your audience?

o   Who is your competition?

o   What differentiates you from your competition?

o   How are you going to reach your audience? (As much as possible, try to break down how you plan to sell your books: What percentage will be bookstore sales, library sales, corporate sales, direct internet sales? How much will each of these distribution channels cost you to implement, and when will you initiate each? You'll be 'guestimating,' but try to predict where you'll devote the bulk of time and energy, and where you have connections. For example, if you're buddies with the CEOs of several major corporations, you can probably safely assume that you'll be doing some significant corporate sales. Be sure to plan to devote at least 50% of your efforts—and to net 50% of your book sales—to non-bookstore markets.

o   How much revenue will each market segment generate?

• Describe your production process: What space requirements, equipment, etc will your publishing house need? (How much will it cost?) Will you require employees, or subcontracting certain parts of the job (such as order fulfillment)?

• Describe your staff. What qualifies you for publishing? Who else will be involved in your publishing house—both staff (including their skills and salary requirements) and freelance advisors (accountant, lawyer, business advisor, etc.)

- Describe briefly your operating procedures: How often will you balance your business accounts and check inventory? Will you have regular meetings with your lawyer or accountant? How often will you review your business operations?

- Plan the bare outlines of your calendar for the next two to five years. Don't panic—this isn't going to be set in stone. But you do need a sense of where you're going—and by when. Include the date you plan to launch your publishing house, how many books you expect to have in publication after each year of business, how much revenue you expect to generate each year, etc.

- For help in writing a business plan, see the interactive workshop at www.AmericanExpress.com, (Select "Small Business" and then "Create a business plan") and the sample business plans at www.BPlans.com. Many business forms are available for free at www.All Business.com.

- Make a note in your calendar (you do have a calendar, don't you?) to check back and review this business plan every six months. You'll be surprised at how useful you will find it if you consult it regularly.

Day Number 5

Today, you'll create a **financial plan**. A financial plan is an important component of the overall business plan, describing when and where money goes in and out of your publishing house.

Create Your Financial Plan

The number-crunching component of your business plan is a financial plan. To hatch a successful business, you need a sound financial plan. Without knowing both what your financial position is, and where you're hoping it will go, it's difficult to get there. Don't think of this step as a boring or scary exercise in math; think of it as your path to publishing success!

- In the beginning, you'll be guessing at a lot of these numbers. Don't worry. It's a worthwhile exercise anyway, and you'll repeat it towards the end of your publishing month, when you'll have a better idea of where you stand. In the meantime, just do the best you can. (A sample budget appears in Appendix B, if you'd like to use those numbers for guidance.)

- We'll break this down into two components: a Profit and Loss Statement and a Cash-Flow Statement. For those of us who somehow missed business school along the way: the Profit and Loss Statement details projected income (from selling books) and expenses (such as utilities and book printing costs); the Cash-Flow Statement shows the daily, weekly, or monthly flow of funds in and out of the business. (Most financial plans also include a balance sheet, which covers business assets, such as equipment, inventory, and monies owed, and debits, such as loans. We'll skip this part for now, because most beginning publishers start with a clean slate.   If you'll be approaching banks or other organizations for a business loan, you will need to include such a balance sheet.)

- Many new entrepreneurs become confused trying to differentiate the cash-flow statement from the profit and loss statement. Consider this simplified example: Let's say the printer wants to charge you $1000 to print the books, and you know you will sell them all and make $5000. Your profit and loss statement will show a profit of $4000. However, the printer wants to be paid right away—not when you sell the books several months later—so even though your profit and loss statement will end the year looking good, your cash-flow statement will show that you have a problem: You need cash to pay the printer before the books sell. See? So you do, in fact, need to keep track of both of these projections. Here's how:

Profit and Loss Statement

Do a projected profit and loss statement for the year. A profit and loss statement is a summary of your finances over a given period of time—in this case, one year—including all income and all operating expenses.

- First, calculate your *gross profit*.

o Calculate projected sales. Include projected book sales (to wholesalers, distributors, online booksellers, web sales, and back-of-room sales at talks), speaking fees, etc. Don't forget to factor in discounts, which can run as high as 68% with an exclusive distributor, 55% with a wholesaler. Deduct your anticipated book returns. This gives you a total number for projected sales. (Just for example, let's say your projected sales are $10,000.)

o Calculate the cost of books sold. (These are the expenses directly connected with the cost of your book, not including items like overhead, which we'll calculate in a moment under operating expenses.) First, add up the cost of book-related expenses, including: editing, cover design, interior book design, indexing, printing, shipping, galleys, and barcode.

Once you have totaled the projected costs for all these items, divide the total expense by the number of books you printed. That will give you the cost per book. Then multiply this per-book cost by the number of books you expect to sell the first year. That gives you the cost of books sold. (For example, if the editing, cover design, printing, etc of your book costs $5,000, and you printed 5,000 books, the per-book cost is $1/book. If you expect to sell 3,000 books this year, then your cost of books sold is $3,000. (Don't worry about the 2,000 books in inventory whose cost you have ignored; that will be factored into next year's cost of books.) If you are considering printing more than 5,000 books, because the per-book cost is so much lower, think again;

you're infinitely better off printing at a slightly higher per-book cost until you are sure you know what you are doing. The biggest mistake small publishers make is to optimistically over-print books. My advice is to start small and then reprint no more than a 6 month supply.

o Finally, calculate *gross profit* by subtracting the projected cost of books sold ($3,000 in our example above) from the projected sales generated during the year. ($10,000 in our example above, giving our example a gross profit of $7,000.) Remember, this does not include operating expenses or taxes.

- Next, calculate your *operating expenses*. These are the everyday expenses associated with running your business, and include the following:

o One-time costs: Telephones, answering machines, computer, printer, fax machine, copier, ISBN block, costs of LLC or incorporation, web design.

o Annual costs: Licenses, LLC fees, insurance, publisher association membership fees, contest entry fees, web hosting, professional magazine subscriptions

o Monthly costs: Rent, utilities, local and long distance telephone bills, salaries, merchant account fees, shopping cart services, fulfillment house, bank fees.

o Random-time costs: Advertising, conferences, travel expenses of attending conferences and talks, publicity (book displays, co-op mailings, BookSense participation, postcards, flyers, mailing lists, review copies), office supplies, and postage, business cards.

- Finally, subtract your projected operating expenses (just for example, let's say all those operating expenses came to $1,000) from your projected gross profit (that was the $7,000 in the previous example, giving you a figure of $6,000) Then adjust this figure by subtracting the taxes you will owe, and the final number is your *net income*.

One other thing to be aware of in calculating profits and expenses is this: At least initially, you need to plan to give books away for review purposes. You will not be earning money on these books. For accounting purposes, it probably makes the most sense to add these costs (the per-book cost multiplied by the number of review copies you plan to give out) to your operating expenses.

Also, remember that bookstores can return books they've purchased, even as long as a year later. Don't spend all your book income until you're sure that the books won't be coming back.

Once you are publishing multiple titles, you should do an annual profit and loss statement for each and every title.

Finally, remember that the profit and loss statement only reflects the money flowing in a particular period of time (in our example, one year) and doesn't take into account income (or inventory) carried over from a previous year. Thus, you will also need to do a cash-flow statement to ascertain the true financial story of your publishing house.

Cash-Flow Statement

Next, you'll do a projected month-by-month cash-flow statement, showing how quickly the money will flow out (for equipment, to printers, etc.) and how quickly it will be replenished (by book sales, etc.) Use the same numbers you used in the profit and loss statement above, but this time, instead of lumping all the income and expenses together, calculate out when you will be paying each bill and receiving each check.

For example, let's say you start your publishing house with $3,000.   The first month in business, you buy a $500 computer and pay $400 for an editor to look over your manuscript. At the end of the first month, your cash-flow will show that you have $2,100.   The second month, you spend $200 on a fax machine, and earn $500 speaking on your new (still-unpublished) book. You end that month with $2,400. And so on.

- Put your variable costs in the month they must be paid.

- Spread your fixed costs out evenly over the year.

- Plan out your entire first year of publishing in this way, to be sure you will have enough cash on hand to pay expenses as they arise. Make sure that each month's totals are positive.   (Otherwise you'll have to cut expenses somewhere.)

- Bear in mind, as you're mapping out your month by month projections, that book revenues will most often be received 90-120 days after the book's sale and invoice (because wholesalers generally get these payment terms.)

- Also, consider that wholesalers often send returns—rather than checks—when their accounts are due, and deduct these credits upon receipt. (Thus, for example, if the wholesaler owes you for 5,000 books, and orders 3,000 more, and then returns the 3,000, they'll deduct it from the 5,000 they owe you right now.) Since you have no way of knowing *which* books they've returned, you will be, in effect, the banker financing the wholesaler's cash flow!

This week you:

- Made sure you wanted to self publish
- Defined your goals
- Zeroed-in on a hot subject
- Defined your target audience
- Chose a title and subtitle for your book
- Wrote the cover copy
- Set the book's price
- Chose a publication date
- Created your financial plan
- Wrote your business plan

Congratulations! You've made a great start!

Week Number Two

ငၓ ၵ

This week you'll:

- Choose a company name
- Choose financial software
- Set up your legal structure
- Learn about the legalities
- Establish your company
- Get an ISBN
- Fill out an ABI
- Set a discount schedule and terms
- Plan your future titles
- Establish your website
- Decide how to sell your books
- Consider Print on Demand

Day Number 6

Today you'll **choose a company name** and **financial software** to run your business.

Choose Your Company Name

The first thing to do is pick a name for your publishing house.

- Many first-time publishers are inclined to use their own name as the name of their publishing house. *Avoid doing this!* When reviewers get a copy of "About Dogs" written by John Smith, published by John Smith Publishing, they will toss your book straight into the wastebasket. Reviewers, the media, and just about everyone in the book business shuns self-publishers; consider yourself, instead, an *independent* publisher.

- Pick a general name, rather than a specific name. "Blueberry Pie Press" might work great for your dessert cookbook, but if your second book is on choosing a divorce lawyer, you may lose sales unnecessarily.

- Try for something at the beginning of the alphabet. That way, your publishing name will appear earlier in directories.

- Be clever, but avoid the temptation to choose a too-cutesy name: There's a fine line between "cute and memorable" and "too cute." If your venture is successful, you may be stuck with "Gummy Bear Press" for a long, long time.

- Make sure that the name is easy to pronounce and spell, so that people can find it easily in listings.

- Make sure you can lock in the domain name for your publishing house's website. Also, be sure that it is the "dot-com" that is available. (If only the "dot-org" is available, pick another name; you can't use a dot-org for a commercial business.) In fact, no one will think to look under anything other than "dot com." Buy the domain name before you commit to the name of the publishing house.

- Check to make sure that no one is using the name you've chosen. Check in current directories such as Literary Market Place (LMP), and also check an old, out of print directory of LMP, to make sure that you haven't chosen the name of a company that's gone out of business; you don't want to encourage receiving someone else's overdue notices. Check the name online also, to make sure it's not in use: Search for it at www.Google.com. And check internet yellow pages such as www.InfoSpace.com and www.Switchboard.com. Also, check the U.S. Patent and Trademark office at tess.uspto.gov or www.NameProtect.com.

Choose Financial Software

Now that you've chosen a company name, consider investing in financial software to keep your business finances organized. You've already done the hard work—creating the business and financial plan. Now you just need a system to keep your numbers organized.

- Good financial software will let you easily document your invoices and accounts receivable; print invoices, packing lists, and mailing labels; keep track of how many copies of titles distributors have in stock; easily compute author royalties; and figure inventory depreciation for your taxes. (Some software also can be used to check the usefulness of various types of promotional activities; assess the impact of color, packaging, and other production details on a title; organize follow-up to reviewers, and maintain a mailing list or customer database.)

- There are three affordable publisher-specific computer programs for small publishers that offer the ability to invoice, send statements, track inventory, track royalties, and generate reports: Publishers Assistant, PUB123, and Fat Boys' Myrlyn. All boast happy users:

  o Publishers Assistant. Steve Carlson, Upper Access, PO Box 457, 85 Upper Access Road, Hinesburg, VT 05461, (800)310-8716, fax (802)482-7730, info@UpperAccess.com, www.PubAssist.com, www.UpperAccess.com. $300-$2,500. Download a free full-working demo and manual at www.PubAssist.com.

  o PUB123. Alan Canton, Adams-Blake Company, 8041 Sierra Street, Fair Oaks, CA 95628, (916)962-9296, info@adams-blake.com, www.Adams-Blake.com

o Myrlyn, Fat Boys Software, 201 Kenwood Meadows Drive, Raleigh, NC 27603, (919)773-2080, www.Myrlyn.com. $249 and up.

o Cat's Pajamas and Acumen are two more publisher-specific programs, though they are unaffordable for most small publishers, at over $10,000 plus maintenance fees.

- The Cat's Pajamas, 12559 Pulver Road, Burlington, WA 98233, (800)827-2287, fax (360)707-5400, info@tcpj.com, www.tcpj.com

- Acumen, CyberWolf, Inc., 1596 Pacheco #203, Santa Fe, NM 87505, (505)983-6463, fax (505)988-2580, sales@CyberWolf.com, www.AcumenBook.com

o Quicken, QuickBooks, Microsoft Money, and Peachtree Complete Accounting are general purpose bookkeeping packages that can track your numbers (Microsoft Money and Quicken offer invoicing, accounts payable, and the simpler single entry bookkeeping, probably sufficient if you are doing your own books; QuickBooks and Peachtree Complete Accounting offer all these features plus inventory, profit and loss statements, accounts receivable, and double entry bookkeeping.

- Peachtree Complete Accounting, 1505 Pavilion Place, Norcross, GA 30093,

(770)724-4000, www.Peachtree.com.
$300.

- Microsoft Money, www.Microsoft.com/money.
  $35.

- Quicken and Quickbooks, Intuit, Inc., 2800 E.
  Commerce Center Plaza, Tucson, AZ   85706,
  (800)446-8848,   www.QuickBooks.com,   www.
  Intuit.com. $200-$500.

o ProVenture's Invoices and Estimates, available at
  Office Depots and similar stores, helps solely with
  invoicing.

- As you continue to operate your publishing house,
  remember to keep your business and personal finances
  separated, and whenever possible, deposit and withdraw
  all your funds to and from one business checking
  account, so you have a record of your business finances
  in one place. Don't forget to keep detailed records of all
  your business expenses so you can calculate deductions
  accurately on your taxes.

- Tracking publishing invoices can be complicated, because
  payments generally aren't made until 90-120 days after a
  sale.   If you don't enjoy handling everything on the
  computer, set up a separate system to track invoices and
  payments: Use a simple three-ring binder to file copies of
  invoices chronologically by due date. That way you'll
  always have an up-to-date record of which companies
  owe you how much.

- Finally, don't forget that your financial plan—and your entire business plan—is a tool for you to use. Update it, and check it often.

Day Number 7

Today you'll **set up your legal structure** and **learn about the legalities.**

Set Up Your Legal Structure

Setting up your publishing house as a business is not very difficult. But you need to do each step, and in the right order, to avoid legal and financial headaches later.

You can set your press up as a corporation, as a partnership, as a limited liability company (LLC), or as a sole proprietorship. A good source of information on these different structures (as well as solid legal information on a variety of topics, including copyrights, trademarks, etc.) is Nolo at www.Nolo.com. There are advantages and disadvantages to each, and details of legal structures change frequently, so please: Check with a lawyer before deciding.

- Standard (or C) Corporations can hire the owner as an employee, so medical insurance is a deductible expense; and they offer liability protection (creditors can't pursue the owner's individual property if the corporation incurs debt), but they also create much, much more paperwork; in addition, both the corporation and salaries are taxed.

- Subchapter S Corporations provide the same liability protection, but not all the medical expense deductions; on the other hand, only the individual (rather than the corporation as well) is taxed, and the paperwork is somewhat less.

- Sole proprietorships, where the business is owned and operated by one individual, are the easiest to set up, but put you at risk if someone ever decides to sue your publishing house, (since you *are* the publishing house in a sole proprietorship, the court can demand your home to pay off debts.) (One idea is to file as a sole proprietor and increase your personal liability insurance—check with your lawyer.)

- General Partnerships are where the business is co-owned, and the actions of any partner can implicate other partners in the responsibility.

- Limited Partnerships feature one general partner with full legal and fiscal responsibility; silent partners have no managerial or financial say, and hence no liability.

- In states that permit it, a limited liability company may offer the best of all worlds: Little paperwork, and less liability (if you are sued for accidental wrongs or contract issues, your house and property are protected). Check with a lawyer to see which is the best option for you.

The procedure I will describe here is how one files as a Limited Liability Company (and procures the related necessary numbers) in the state of Massachusetts. The procedure varies slightly from state to state, so use this as your guideline, and get the exact details from your local state offices.

o Bear in mind that most states require you to list one manager of the LLC, and two members (one of whom can also be the manager.) You also will need to use a real street address for the LLC, not your post office box. Costs for filing as an LLC are generally around $500, less in states such as Delaware.

- First, procure a federal employer id number. (You want IRS Form SS-4: Application for Employer Identification Number from the Internal Revenue Service; call your local IRS office and ask them to send the form, or check its availability online. In some states, once you have the form you can file over the telephone.) Be sure to write "For ID purposes only" on the form, so that the IRS doesn't assume you have employees and ask you to file quarterly employee reports. Once you have a federal employer id number, your company, rather than you personally, can earn income, possess a bank account, etc.

- With your Employer Identification Number firmly in hand, obtain and fill out IRS Form TA-1. This will involve a trip to yet another government office, to trade the completed form in for a Sales and Use Tax Registration and a Sales Tax Resale Certificate (ST-4) which will enable you to get your books printed without paying sales tax (twice). (You photocopy the ST-4 form and send it to anyone from whom you are receiving goods, to avoid paying the sales tax as a middleman.) There is a minimal fee for this ($10 in Massachusetts.)

- Then, file a ST-9A, Annual Sales and Use Tax Return. (Expect, for the purposes of this form, your sales tax liability to be under their $100 minimum; it's much easier than the alternative options. You can always adjust it later if you end up with a greater sales tax burden. Remember, you only need to collect tax on sales to individuals (retail sales) within your own state; sales out of state are exempt from state tax, and sales to wholesalers are exempt (because the tax is levied further on down the line, at the retail level.)

- With your next set of taxes, file Form 1065.

- File as an LLC. You'll need a "Certificate of Organization" form; you can usually get this from the LLC filing office (which varies from state to state) or from any lawyer.

- Don't forget to refile the LLC every year you're in business. Many states neglect to send out reminder notices, so put this on your calendar; if you forget to refile, you will endanger your reduced liability status.

- Another alternative is to avoid the LLC completely and simply file what is called a "Doing Business As—DBA" at your local county clerk's office or city hall. (Get the blank DBA form at a stationery store; bring it to a notary public to have your signature notarized; then return it to city hall. Be sure to get a few extra, certified copies of your DBA.) A DBA only allows you to do things like open a bank account in your publishing house name. It does not confer legal protection the way an LLC should. Speak with a publishing lawyer for more advice on your particulars.

- Once you have your LLC or DBA, apply for a post office box and bank account in the name of your publishing house. You will need your legal paperwork for this. (If you have filed for a DBA, you may also be required to publish a tiny ad in the local newspaper saying so; check with your county clerk to see if it's required in your county.)

Remember, none of this is legal advice, and everything should be checked with your attorney. All publishing houses have different situations and all states have different rules and requirements; check with an attorney to make sure this advice is right for you.

Learn About the Legalities

Here are some other legalities to consider; there are many more:

- Be sure you sign work-for-hire contracts with your cover designer and editor (and, indeed, with anyone who is doing work on your book). You'll want to use your cover art on items other than your cover—your website, your postcards and flyers, etc. But without a valid work-for-hire contract, your cover designer can legally require you to pay royalties each time you use the graphic. (Yes— even though you've paid for the cover art! This is definitely an area where spending the money on a lawyer and contract beforehand can save you much money and aggravation later on.)

- Be sure you sign a legal contract with your distributor, and be sure that it covers both territories involved and the length of your agreement. In addition, be certain it covers what happens in the event of bankruptcy, and how you will be compensated.

- Know that invoices can be considered a legal contract, and have a lawyer vet yours to be sure it is worded correctly.

- Be sure you speak with a lawyer if you are planning to incorporate others' material into your books. Copyright law is fairly murky, and intellectual property suits can be expensive. Under federal law, you must have written permission to use someone else's work, which includes the use of not only writing but also illustrations, photographs, and other material. You must have written permission whether or not the material contains a copyright notice; whether or not you quote part or all of the material; whether or not you found the material online (even anonymously) on a list or website; whether or not you give credit to the author. Check with a lawyer.

- Not all towns have zoning regulations that allow for operating a business out of your home. Although many small publishers operate under the 'don't ask, don't tell' policy when it comes to announcing their business to their city officials, it's legally safer to find out what the law is in your town.) Local zoning laws may affect your ability to put up signs advertising your business, the percentage of space in your home you're allowed to use for a business, and storage of books on your premises.

You may need a business license, a home occupation permit, a seller's permit, or a building permit.

- It is advisable to speak to a publishing lawyer before setting up your business (or indeed, doing anything involving legal issues: It's always cheaper and easier to get preventative legal advice up front, rather than hiring a lawyer to solve a problem afterwards. Below are a few suggestions for legal sites to consult before starting your business:

  o The Publishing Law Center is run by publishing lawyer Lloyd L. Rich. Packed with useful information, articles posted include information on mergers and acquisitions, internet law, electronic rights, copyright, trademarks, contracts, fair use and right of publicity, privacy, and more. Publishing Law Center, 1163 Vine Street, Denver, CO 80206, (303)388-5215, www.PubLaw.com

  o Ivan Hoffman is a publishing lawyer whose website also houses a wealth of legal information. Ivan@IvanHoffman.com, www.IvanHoffman.com

  o Jonathan Kirsch is an attorney specializing in publishing law, who serves as pro bono general counsel for the Publishers Marketing Association. He is the author of *Kirsch's Handbook of Publishing Law* and *Kirsch's Guide to the Book Contract*. He can be reached at JK@JonathanKirsch.com.

  o Larry Zerner at www.ZernerLaw.com offers a wealth of related links on copyrights, trademarks, and more.

- o Lloyd Jassin is co-author of *Copyright Permission and Libel Handbook: A Step-by-Step Guide for Writers, Editors and Publishers.* Check out his articles on copyright law at www.CopyLaw.com or contact him at 1560 Broadway #400, New York, NY 10036, (212)354-4442, Jassin@CopyLaw.com.

- o You can find sample legal forms of all sorts at www.SearchBug.com/legal/forms2.asp.

- Ascertain whether your company name is already trademarked. (If it is, pick another name; if it isn't, consider trademarking it yourself.) Trademark Express is one company that will run a name through a national search and give you a printed report on whether the name is in use, along with an attorney's opinion on whether you should use it. $175 and up. www.TMExpress.com. Or you can register with the federal Patent and Trademark office directly, at www.USPTO.gov.

- While you're considering legalities, you might also want to consider publishers' liability (also called "media perils") insurance.

  - o Publishers' liability insurance can protect you against intellectual property, libel, copyright infringement, trademark infringement, slander, and defamation claims. It can also protect against invasion of privacy, unfair competition, and misappropriation of ideas. Some policies also protect against bodily injury and property damage claims (if, for example, someone hurts themselves or their house following your directions.)

o In comparing policies, ask about the type of claims covered, the time period covered, the deductible, the coverage limit, and conditions for coverage.

o Check with a knowledgeable lawyer to make sure you're getting the coverage that's right for you. At a minimum, remember to ask if the policy you are considering covers:

▪ Legal fees: Is the insurance company required to defend lawsuits against you? And, separately, are *you* required by the policy to hire a lawyer to review each manuscript? These costs can add up.

▪ Punitive damages: Though some states don't permit punitive damages, punitive damages can be quite expensive.

▪ Different versions: Does the policy cover the hardcover, softcover, audio and online versions of the work? Does it cover press releases, advertising, catalog copy, and workshops on the material?

▪ Different locations: Does the policy cover claims outside, or just inside, the U.S.? (Will your books be sold or distributed in other countries? If so, you'll need coverage in those places.)

• Here are some options for publishers liability coverage:

o PMA and SPAN members can get affordable coverage through Mike Mansel, Argo Insurance Group, 2300 Contra Costa Boulevard #375, Pleasant

Hills, CA 94523, (925)671-5100 x119, fax (925)658-1601, mikem@publiability.com, www.Pub Liability.com.

o ABA members can get coverage through Patrick Haller, Publisher Insurance Program Manager, Libris, (866)542-7471, PHaller@RiskCap.com. Annual premiums are based on gross revenues; coverage includes publisher professional errors and omissions, slander, copyright infringement, etc. Coverage limits up to $10 million; deductibles start at $2,500. A.M. Best Rating of A+. www.Libris.org

o Small Press Center members can get coverage through Media/Professionals Insurance. For more information, call (816)292-7207, or see the Small Press website at www.SmallPress.org.

o The National Writers Union typically offers affordable coverage, though recently they have had difficulty with their carrier. Check the latest at www.NWU.org.

Day Number 8

Today you'll **establish your company, get an ISBN**, set a **discount schedule and terms**, and **plan your future titles**.

Establish Your Company

Here are some of the things you'll need to do to establish your publishing house:

- Open a bank account. Bring along your legal papers certifying your business is a corporation or partnership. Put your press name, address, telephone, and email address on your business checks for ease of use. Be sure you keep your business checking account separate from your personal account. You should also get a separate business credit card, to keep business purchases separated. While you're at it, get a rubber stamp with the deposit information for your business bank account, so that when the checks start rolling in you can easily endorse them for deposit. (The stamp should say, "For Deposit Only to Account of (Publishing House Name)" followed by the bank account number and your business address and telephone number.

- Obtain a post office box. (I recommend doing it at the post office, as opposed to one of the private mail-drop services, for the simple reason that if the private service goes out of business or relocates, you'll have to reprint all your business cards, brochures, books—everything that had the now-erroneous address.) I also recommend getting a post office box instead of (or in addition to) using a street address. If you should move, the post office will only forward your street address mail for one year. (You can, however, keep your post office box forever.)

- Get a separate business telephone line. Nobody knows if they've called a corporate office filled with secretaries or you at home in your bathrobe—unless your four-year-old answers the telephone. Spend the money on a separate business line. Also, make sure your business number is listed, so that other businesses can find you.

  o Check out www.UReach.com which offers the ability to send and receive telephone calls, voicemail, faxes, and email via an 800 number.

  o Look at Unitel (800/499-5912) which offers competitively-priced long distance service.

  o For a comparison of the latest telephone company plans, check out www.ABellTolls.com.

- Consider getting a separate (phone or high-speed internet access) line for internet access, so your business phone line won't be busy for long stretches of time.

- Print business cards. You can print stationery and brochures on your printer these days, but at least your business cards should be professionally printed: It's very inexpensive and looks much more professional. To really make a splash, put the cover of your book on the business card. Include your email address and website.

(`SeraphMedia.com` offers 1000 for $30, including delivery.)

- Purchase printer paper, envelopes, stamps, and shipping envelopes (to send your books out for review.) Rubber stamps that say "Paid" and "Requested Material" can be useful in processing invoices and sending out media requests respectively.

- If your publishing house is going to be your livelihood, you need to read some business books on owning and operating a home business, beyond the scope of this book. Two quick tips: Check out the home-based business links at `www.BizOffice.com` and info on affordable health insurance at `www.EHealthInsurance` `.com`.

- In the future, consider a dedicated fax line. (Don't list your fax number, however—listing it will increase the number of junk mail faxes you receive.) If you don't want to shell out extra for a separate fax line, you can get one free at `www.EFax.com`. (You'll get an email telling you when you have a fax to download.) `www.FaxaWay.com` lets you fax via your email, without having to shell out for a fax machine. Check out the possibilities of a fax-back system (that will let callers get catalogs and other information automatically) at `www.Copia.com/FaxFacts/papers/Fax-on-Demand` `.htm`.

Get an ISBN

All books that will be sold to libraries and bookstores require an ISBN. ISBN stands for International Standard Book Number. The ISBN is a worldwide identification system for books and ensures that books are identified, ordered, and shipped correctly. R. R. Bowker is the U.S. registry of ISBNs, and the only place in the U.S. to get an ISBN. (In Canada, go through the National Library of Canada.) Here's how to get an ISBN for your book, as well as some more details you'll need to know about ISBNs:

- Bookstores and libraries—as well as wholesalers and distributors—require each book to have an ISBN for identification purposes.

- You'll need the ISBN when (on Day Number 12) you're ready to order a barcode for the book's back cover. The barcode includes both the ISBN and scanning information.

- Each version of the material needs a unique ISBN. That means you'll need a separate ISBN for the hardcover, softcover, audio, video and e-book versions of the book.

- The ISBN appears on both the back cover of the book (above or below the bar code) and on the copyright page of the book.

- All ISBNs are ten digits, composed of four groups of numbers, separated by dashes. The first digit indicates the country of origin: An initial "1" or "0" means the book was published in an English speaking country. The next group of (5, 6, or 7) digits identifies the publisher:

Each publisher has a unique number. The third group of (1, 2, or 3) digits identifies the book itself. The last single digit is a check digit which ensures that the other digits are correct; if a clerk inadvertently transposes or mistypes digits, the check digit alerts them to their error. (*X* as the check digit is used instead of 10.)

o The calculation is based on a modulus 11, and you can check your own ISBN number easily. Multiply each of the digits of your ISBN by a number ranging from 10 to 1, in descending order, and then add products. Thus, the digits for this book's ISBN (1-893290-85-9) are multiplied by digits from 10 to 1, and the resulting products are added:

```
1-893290-85-9

x 10-987654-32-1

----------------

10+72+72+21+12+45+0+24+10+9 = 275
```

Divide this sum (275) by 11 (275/11) which is 25. The result must be a whole number, with no remainder, for the ISBN to be valid.

• You can't order just one ISBN from Bowker: You must order a block of 10, 100, or 1000. They charge $225 for ten ISBNs, and a whopping $800 for 100 ISBNs. (New publishers always ask if there's any way to buy just one ISBN. The answer is an unequivocal NO. The smallest block you can buy from Bowker is a block of ten numbers.) Also, keep in mind that the owner of the ISBN number is the publisher-of-record for the book—

so even if you could find another publisher willing to sell you a single ISBN number, that would identify their publishing house—not yours—as the publisher of the book. (They would then receive the orders, the returns, the checks—you get the idea. If you give or sell one of your ISBN numbers to someone else, you are the publisher of record if they are sued for copyright violation, libel, etc.) This is not the place to cut corners; buy your own ISBNs. Since you need a different ISBN for each version of the work, you'll need more ISBNs than you may think, anyway—a different one for hardcover, softcover, audio, and e-book editions.

- Unfortunately, everyone in the publishing industry can tell how many ISBNs you have purchased by examining your ISBN. (Publishers with five digits in their second block of numbers have purchased 1000; publishers with six digits have purchased 100; and publishers with seven digits have purchased only ten ISBNs.) Purchasing only ten ISBNs signals that you are a one-or-two book publisher. If you want to present yourself as a serious independent publisher, as opposed to a one-book self-published author, you'll need to go for one of the larger, more expensive blocks.

- Request the ISBN application form from R. R. Bowker, 630 Central Avenue, New Providence, NJ 07974, (908)771-7755, fax (908)665-2895, isbn-san@bowker .com, www.isbn.org.

- In Canada, request the ISBN form from Canadian ISBN Agency, The National Library of Canada, 395 Wellington

Street, Ottawa, ON   K1A-0N4, (819) 994-6872, fax
(819)997-7517, isbn@NLC-Bnc.ca, www.nlc-bnc.ca.

- Bowker's turn-around time for ISBNs is ten business days
from receipt of the completed form. Once they process
your order, Bowker will send you a few pages of
numbers, which is referred to as a "logbook." Every time
you publish a new book—or a new version—you assign it
an ISBN and write it into your logbook.

- Don't start assigning ISBNs with the first number in your
logbook. (The first number ends in a "0" which will
signal that it is your first book.) Pick a number randomly
from the middle of your ISBN logbook. Consider saving
consecutive ISBNs for different versions of the same
product.

- Keep in mind that whenever you reprint your title—
regardless of a price change—you must maintain the
original ISBN, according to Bowker. So don't plan to just
put in any old price here with the idea of changing the
price down the road; once you file for this ISBN, you're
committed to the data.

- Some publishers also purchase a SAN from Bowker.
SAN stands for Standard Address Number, and identifies
the different mailing addresses of multi-location
companies. Unless your publishing house has multiple
addresses for billing and shipping, you can safely skip this
step. A SAN costs $125 and can be purchased by
emailing ISBN-SAN@Bowker.com.

- If you have any questions or problems with your ISBNs, email Bowker at isbn-san@Bowker.com.

- If you're planning to sell your book in drugstores and grocery stores, you will also need a Price Point UPC (Universal Product Code) with ISBN Add On barcode. In the same way that the ISBN and barcode are required for selling your book to bookstores and libraries, the UPC manufacturer's identification number and UPC barcode are required for selling your book in other retail outlets. For more information on UPC, contact the Uniform Code Council, 7887 Washington Village Drive #300, Dayton, OH   45459, (937)435-3870, fax (937)435-7317, www.UCCouncil.org.

Fill Out an ABI

As soon as you have your ISBN, fill out an ABI.

- ABI is R.R. Bowker's Advance Book Information form. All books announced via ABI are listed in Bowker's *Books in Print*. Since *Books in Print* is used heavily by many in the book industry, it is definitely worthwhile to fill out an ABI.

- Barnes & Noble recently announced that it would use Bowker's Books in Print as its sole database for all chain stores as well as for Barnes & Noble.com, making this an essential step.

- There's no charge for the ABI service once you have ISBN numbers.

- One bit of information you'll need for the ABI form is your official publication date. Bear in mind that what they're asking for is *not* the date you get books from the printer. What they want to know is your *official* publication date. Traditional approaches suggest filling out the ABI a full six months before the books will be printed. Certainly you should ensure that you submit the ABI early enough so that reviewers can find your title listed in *Forthcoming Books in Print* while they're considering writing your review. Refer back to the section on choosing a publication date (page 41) for more details.

- The item about STOP discount on the ABI form is covered in the following section.

- Remember to fill out two separate forms (with unique ISBNs) if you are planning on both a hardcover and softcover edition.

- You can fill out the ABI form in hardcopy, by requesting forms from R.R. Bowker, 630 Central Avenue, New Providence, NJ 07974, (908)771-7755, fax (908)665-2895.

- Or fill out the ABI online at www.BowkerLink.com. Click on "Add/Update in Books in Print." If you are already registered at BowkerLink, enter your username and password, and click on "login." Otherwise, click on "register" and follow the directions. Your username and password will be emailed to you within three days. Every time you want to add a new title, sign in, click on "Add Item" and enter the required information.

- Be aware that you can now pay for an enhanced listing (some printed information describing your book) as well as a cover image to be added to your Books in Print listing. Contact DataAcquisition@Bowker.com for more details. Some publishers advocate that this enhanced listing is worthwhile (because it enables librarians to give patrons more information on titles); others argue that they won't be seeing your annotation anyway unless they're already looking for your book.

- Another new service is the ability through Bowker's new Title Express service to have your listing sent to anyone you would like. Contact Data Sales Manager Al Caro at Al.Caro@Bowker.com.

Set a Discount Schedule and Terms

You will need to decide on a discount schedule and terms. Here are some things to consider:

- You can offer one set of terms to wholesalers, and another set of terms to retailers, but according to federal law (the Robinson-Patman Act) you are legally required to offer the same terms to comparable outlets within a category; thus, if you offer one wholesaler a certain discount, you must offer *all* wholesalers that discount. You have some flexibility in that you can set different terms based on quantities purchased—for example, "55% discount on orders of 40 books or more; 40% discount on orders of fewer than 40 books."

- "Standard" terms of wholesalers are 55% discount (that is, you retain only 45% of the retail price of the book); you pay shipping of orders (to the wholesaler) and shipping of returns (when they send books back); all books are sold on consignment (that is, the books can be returned to you at any time and for any reason); and they will send payment in 90 (which usually means at least 120) days. Standard discounts to exclusive distributors are upwards of 65%.

- You don't have to agree to the standard terms. You can offer less than the 55% discount (some publishers set their discount schedule at 20%); insist that they pay shipping via Fed Ex Ground collect or UPS collect in one or both directions; sell books non-returnable, rather than on consignment; and demand prepayment for all orders. Or, you can agree to standard terms on some issues, and set your own terms on others: It's up to you to decide which issues are most important to you and which terms you can live with.

- If you are going to apply to the Baker & Taylor program through SPAN, you must accept B&T's standard terms— 55% discount and returnability. So consider this carefully before you apply.

- In thinking about discount terms, one trick is to set the price of your book high enough that you can easily *afford* 55% discount. (All my titles, for example, are priced between $14.95 and $24.95, and that gives me enough slack to offer 55% terms to my largest buyers.)

- Understand that wholesalers will order anything that the bookstores or libraries request, *regardless of your terms.* While it is true that *bookstores* might be reluctant to order a book which is non-returnable, as long as bookstores and libraries order it, wholesalers will stock it. That means that as long as you are generating sufficient demand for your book by readers, you don't have to worry about your terms being unacceptable to the wholesalers.

- Consider the sample budget in Appendix B (and review the discussion on setting book prices in Week 1) to help in figuring out how much your publishing venture will cost, and what sorts of discount terms you can afford.

- Plan what you want your STOP discount to be. STOP stands for Single Title Order Plan, and refers to the discount you offer to retail stores who are buying single copies of your book (almost always in direct response to a customer's request.)

    o The bookstore will simply send you a check (discounted the specified amount); you ship the book and there's no more paperwork involved.

    o Most publishers set their STOP at 20% discount plus shipping. There's no particular reason to give a larger discount; STOP orders do not usually lead to larger orders, so don't set a higher discount in the hope of making big sales.

    o Once you've figured out your STOP terms, go back and fill in this section of the Bowker ABI.

o Also send your STOP terms directly to the American Booksellers Association (ABA) for inclusion in the ABA Book Buyers Handbook, which is now fully searchable online and used by bookstores nationwide to fulfill customer requests. Officially, the ABA requires your publishing house to be a year old and have published at least three titles, which is why you'll need the list of forthcoming titles in the next section. Although they have traditionally listed publishers who are not ABA members, it's possible that this policy is changing. In the meantime, send them both your list of "Forthcoming Titles" and "Terms" and ask to be included. See www.news.Bookweb.org/read/614 for more details or write to: American Booksellers Association, 828 South Broadway, Tarrytown, NY 10591, (800)637-0037, fax (914)591-2720, www.Book Web.org.

• Finally, on your publishing house letterhead, type up a list entitled "Terms" including your discounts for various quantities, etc. You'll send this to wholesalers and use it for inclusion in certain directories later.

Plan Your Future Titles

It may seem preposterous to be planning future titles now—you've just barely started on your first title!—but in order to successfully publish this book, that's what you need to do. There are two reasons for this. One is that, unfortunately, many sectors of the publishing industry—including, but not limited to, Ingram, The Library of Congress, and Bowker—won't take you seriously when you're starting out as a publisher. To get around this problem, you're going to need to publish a list of forthcoming titles, to give your publishing house the image of being larger.

The second reason is that, in order to run a publishing company, you need to occupy a specific editorial niche. To do this successfully, you need to have a vision of the titles *after* this one—and be sure these titles fit into your unique niche. Consider both the subject matter and the approach.

Once you've considered your future titles, here's what to do:

- Type up a formal letter, on your publishing house letterhead, that says, "Forthcoming titles from (name of your press.)"

- List each title that you plan to produce in the next ten years. (Yes, *ten* years.) Include the name of the author, the page count, the editions (hardcover, softcover, or both?) and the retail price. (None of this information is binding, so just estimate as best you can.) After you get your ISBN block from Bowker, you will assign an ISBN number to each title as well.

- Now, with several forthcoming titles firmly in hand, you're eligible for a wide array of programs that exclude smaller presses or self-publishers. Include this list when you're contacting:

    o Ingram (about being carried by this wholesaler); see Day Number 10.

    o The Library of Congress (when you apply for cataloging in publication data); see Week Number

Four. (The Library of Congress officially does not care how many titles you publish, but they do not catalog titles of publishers who publish only one author, which is considered self-publishing.)

o Bowker, and particularly Literary Market Place (LMP); to be listed in this important annual directory, they require publishers to produce at least three new titles annually.

o The American Booksellers Association Book Buyers' Handbook (which bookstores use to order single titles directly that have been requested by a customer; the Book Buyers Handbook requires at least three titles if you want to be listed.)

Day Number 9

Today you'll get started **creating your website.**

Create Your Website

Whether or not you're going to do your own book distribution (discussed extensively in the next section) you should create a website. A website offers more than just the capability for people to buy your book. It's an advertisement for your book and publishing house; a show-case for your media inquiries; and a convenient source of information for readers who are interested in your products. Here's how to get started on developing a quality website; if you're planning to do your own book distribution, you'll also need to examine tomorrow's tasks on setting up credit card transactions.

- If you want your business to look professional, you absolutely need your own domain name (For example, YourBusiness.com.) Many beginners start by signing up with a service that offers free web pages—but if you do that, your site will have a name like AngelFire.com/YourBusiness or Members.aol.com/ YourBusiness/. Using an online mall will similarly limit your professional appearance. Spring for the extra professionalism your own domain name offers. Register your name with wwwNetworkSolutions.com. ($70/2 year license of the name.) Be sure to register the "dot-com" domain name, at the very least. You can find out easily if your preferred domain name is available at `https://www.netsol.com/cgi-bin/whois/whois`.

- Select an ISP (internet service provider). The most well-known ISPs include AOL, Earthlink, AT&T, MSN and Mindspring, but there are thousands of others.

- Sign up for a web hosting plan. Most offer a choice of tools with which to design your site. Check out a ranked list of web hosting companies: go to `www.WebHost List.com`, click on "Hosting." Read the article "How to pick the right Web host for your site" for good tips on choosing a web hosting company. Also check the "Top 25" listings at `www.hostindex.com`. Popular web hosts include:

  o `www.Hostway.com` (our current favorite)

  o `www.Affinity.com`

  o `www.Webmasters.com`

  o `www.Earthlink.net`

  o `www.Verio.com`

  o `www.BigBiz.com`

  o `www.ApolloHosting.com`

  o `www.ImageLinkUsa.net`

If you suddenly hit it really big, and your website gets flooded with so many requests that your web host can't handle it, contact Akamai (`www.akamai.com`), which can copy your web site to machines all around the world; when a customer requests one of your web pages, it comes from the closest such machine. In emergencies, they can get your site "mirrored" in a day.

- To design the actual website, you might find it easiest to use a design package that has a what-you-see-is-what-you-get editor, so you won't have to learn to code in HTML. Use the templates provided by your web host, or one of the web design software packages on the market. You can research which design package is for you at www.zdnet.com or www.cnet.com which review these tools. These are among the most popular web design packages:

  o Macromedia Dreamweaver (not for beginners)

  o Adobe GoLive (not for beginners)

  o NetObjects Fusion

  o Microsoft FrontPage

- You may find the following sites helpful in designing your website:

  o www.WebDesign.about.com

  o www.Toolsforthe.net

  o www.graphic-design.com/Web/

- In designing your site, keep in mind the following:

  o Be sure to view your site using different browsers—or ask a friend to help do this. What looks good on your screen may not look great in someone else's browser.

  o Keep download time to a minimum. Download time is dependent on the viewer's computer, but it also depends on the number (keep it to just a few) and the size (keep them small) of your graphics. (You may need to reduce your book cover image size and quality to make it display faster. In most cases, you can right-click on the image and select *Properties* and *Dimensions* to reduce file size. Graphics development tools for the web often contain automatic image optimizers that reduce image size.)

o   Keep your web pages narrow, so viewers using a smaller screen width won't have to scroll right or left to see everything, which can get really annoying very quickly.

o   Be sure that your pages have different titles so that the search engines index all the pages. (Change the *page titles* and keep the titles to six words or fewer.)

o   Stay away from moving graphics. Some people hate them.

o   Be sure to check out www.SearchEngineWatch.com for suggestions on placement, submissions to search engines, etc. This is very important: If you want people to be able to find your site, it **must** appear in the first page of sites returned by search engines when people search for sites related to your book's topic.

o   Try the free online 7-week email/autoresponder course in Search Engine Optimization Strategies. www.BoogieJack.com/seos.html

• If you're not interested in getting into web design, hire someone. (Just be sure that the domain name is registered in the name of your business, not theirs.) The following people and businesses are experienced in designing websites for publishers; the first three listings also offer web hosting packages:

o Eric Anderson, Future Thru Group, supplies web instruction so you can easily design and maintain your own site. Price of $950 includes web design and one year of complimentary hosting. 135 Rugg Avenue, Newark, OH 43055, (740)501-1058, www.Future Thru.com

o BookZone. Hosting packages start with single title listings at $109 per year through more comprehensive packages starting at $700 per year plus a $350 set up fee. Contact them at BookZone, PO Box 9642, Scottsdale, AZ 85252, (800)536-6162, fax (480)481-0103, Bookzone@Bookzone.com

o Site Build It. Hosting packages include site design tools, search engine optimization, and domain registration. $300 per year. www.SiteSell.com

o Amy Lewis at Digital Drone Studios. $35/hour; web pages generally take between 1-2 hours to design. (720)494-7813, www.DigitalDrone.net

o Jill Katz at Katz & Mouse. (805)899-3001, fax (413)383-8072, Jill@KatzAndMouse.com, www. Katzandmouse.com

• One other solution is the new low-cost website hosting offered by the national writing organization, the Author's Guild. The program is open to both members and nonmembers of the Author's Guild, though participants are required to have been professionally published. A single-page listing costs $3 per month; a standard site, with up to ten titles, is $6 per month; a larger site (with up to 50 titles) is only $9 per month. The Author's Guild will also register your domain name for $18/year and provide email for an additional $3. Fees include submission of sites to major search engines, and promotion. They do not offer order-taking capabilities at this time. 31 East 28ᵗʰ Street, 10ᵗʰ Floor, New York, NY 10016-7396, www.AuthorsGuild.net

- Once your website is up, be sure to get it listed so that people can find it. Many web hosting companies offer basic search-engine submission services for free. Also check out the following sites for help (for a fee) in listing with the major search engines:

  o www.SiteAnnounce.com

  o www.Submit-It.com

  o www.JimTools.com

  o www.SearchEngineWatch.com

- If you're planning to take book orders on your website (or in person) see the extensive details in the next section.

Day Number 10

Today, you'll think about **how to sell** your books. This looks like way too much work for one day—but it's mostly making the decision as to which distribution method will work best for you. The actual tasks, no matter which way you decide, are not too many.

Decide How to Sell Your Books

While this is a big topic (**The Publishing Game: Bestseller in 30 Days** is one of many books devoted to this subject) there are a few important decisions you need to make now. Will you:

- Sell to bookstores and libraries

  o Through an exclusive distributor?

  o Through a Print on Demand publisher?

  o Through a wholesaler?

- Sell directly to consumers

  o Through a website?

  o Through a Print on Demand publisher?

  o Through your own lectures and classes?

- Or (most commonly) some combination of the above?

The next sections examine each of these options.

Distribution Options

In many ways, the publishing business is a constant chicken-and-egg problem. Distributing your books is just one example. You can't get a distributor or wholesaler until you have orders for a book—but how do you get orders before you have a book? And how do you do a book until you've decided how you'll distribute it? It's quite the conundrum, and it doesn't help that the rules seem to keep changing. Here's how to tackle it:

Decide About Print on Demand

The first thing that you need to decide is how much of the project you want to do yourself. The buzz words in the publishing industry these days are POD—print on demand. Everyone's doing it, thinking about doing it, talking about the advantages and disadvantages of doing it. There's a lot of confusion, even amongst publishing mavens, about what Print On Demand is, and is not, and when one should use it. Here's what you need to know about Print on Demand:

- First of all, the phrase "Print on Demand" refers to two different things. (There is much argument within the industry as to which of these is the "correct" use of POD, but both are used, causing much confusion.)

  o POD Printers: The first usage is POD as a means of production or printing. It is a production method by which small publishers or individuals can print small quantities of books. The traditional printing presses (offset printers) need to print in large quantities (of at least 1,000) to make the printing costs of each book cost-effective; but by using a digital printer, similar to a copying machine, you can print one or a few books at a time in a cost-effective manner. Bear in mind that POD per-unit costs will always be higher than standard printing: Printing 3,000 copies of a 200-page book traditionally might cost you $2.00 per book; POD printers might charge $4.50 to $5 per book. (But you will have the option to print 100 instead of 3,000 copies; you're trading off higher per-unit costs with lower capital investment and less inventory management.)   In this context, POD just means you've printed a small quantity of books on a digital printer, rather than a larger quantity of books via traditional (offset) printing press. This usage of POD doesn't have any connotations of who will handle the book production or marketing; it is simply a way to describe printing in small quantities. A POD printer charges a set price to print your book, and that's the beginning and end of your relationship.   POD printers function just like any other printer, except for the difference in quantity produced and difference in price (the up-front costs are lower, but the per-book price is higher, making it cost-effective only for small quantities.)   The quality of POD printing is also variable, depending on the printer you choose. Choosing a POD printer can be useful if you want to:

- Send just a few copies to review journals (and wait until you see the reviews before deciding to print more)

- Test the waters to see how the books do in the marketplace

- Float several versions of the same book to see which title/size/design draws the most customers

- Produce a small quantity of a book for a particular niche sale or as a premium or gift for a client or corporation

- Fulfill a few remaining or sudden orders for a book that you retired or that has gone out of print

- Keep your inventory (and warehousing headaches, and of course total cash outlay) lower overall

o Many traditional printers also do POD printing: A complete list is included on Day Number 24. A few POD printers with good prices are:

- DeHart's, 3265 Scott Boulevard, Santa Clara, CA 95054, (888)982-4763, fax (408)982-9912, www.De Harts.com

- Fidlar Doubleday, Inc., 6255 Technology Avenue, Kalamazoo, MI 49009, (800)632-2259, fax (866) 398-9655, www.Fidlar.com

- Lightning Source, 1246 Heil Quaker Boulevard, LaVergne, TN 37086, (615)213-5815, www. LightningSource.com

- Offset Paperback Manufacturers, Studio Print Group, 101 Memorial Highway, Dallas, PA 18612, (570)675-5261, www.opm.com

- One2One, 27460 Avenue Scott, Valencia, CA 91355, (661)702-9000, fax (661)702-9001, www.121Direct.net

- Quebecor World, 1989 Arcata Boulevard, Martinsburg, WV 25402, (304)267-3600, fax (304)267-0989, www.QuebecorWorld.com

- R. R. Donnelley Paper Solutions, 77 West Wacker Drive, Chicago, IL 60601, (312)326-8000, www.RRDonnelley.com

○ To POD print 200 copies of a 208-page paperback book with a competitively-priced POD printer will average between $2.75 and $5.50, depending on the POD printer selected. (Note that using a POD printer at the high end of that range will cost you $1,100 for your 200 copies; your alternative would be a traditional printer, which shouldn't run you more than $2,000 for 1,000 copies. Be sure you have carefully considered your quantities and price points.)

○ POD Publishers: The second usage refers to the myriad of companies that have sprouted like wildflowers calling themselves POD publishers. These companies publish your book for you, for a minimal investment. Some of them print the books only as they are ordered (as in "on demand"); others print small quantities of the books (as do the POD printers.) Unlike a POD printer (which just charges you for the cost of the books) once you have paid a POD publisher the initial outlay (which can buy you internal and cover design, ISBN and barcode, *Books in Print* listing, and listings on Amazon and BarnesAnd Noble.com) you get a percentage or royalty (which varies by POD publisher) of the retail price of the book. In many ways, these companies straddle the fence between small publishing and vanity publishing. (Vanity publishers are companies that will publish *any* book for an [usually] exorbitant fee.) Consider the following if you are considering using a POD publisher to do your book:

- Many POD publishers insist on using their own ISBN; others will let you use your own.) If they retain the ISBN, then you have little control over the book should you end up displeased with the company; orders will still go to them, and they will, in effect, "own" the book even though you will retain the copyright. On the other hand, if you use your own ISBN, orders will come to you when they should go to the POD company. Neither is a particularly happy situation.

- Most, but not all, of these POD publishers format the interiors of the books, design the covers, and (possibly) do some editing. Depending on the quality of the POD publisher's work, this can either improve or harm the book's integrity and sales. (Many of the major POD publishers now use the same backend company to print the books—Lightning Source, a division of Ingram—so at least among the major players, print quality is consistent. You can also utilize Lightning Source yourself as a POD printer.)

- POD books don't do photos well; photos do not reproduce well printed digitally. If your book requires good photo quality, stick to offset (traditional) printing. Photos printed digitally will also require more toner, and thus may add to the final price of the printing.

- Spine fitting may be affected by POD printing; check with your printer to make sure that the spine width you used for your offset book will still fit if the book is printed digitally.

- Most of the POD publishers charge some sort of up-front fee (approximately $500) for their time and effort, and pay the author a "royalty" percentage on retail sales (of around 20-25% of *net* revenue, rather than retail price.)

- Although the initial setup costs of POD publishers are quite low, the ongoing unit costs (that is, the per book costs) are disproportionately high. If your $10 book costs $5 to produce, you will *not* be able to sell it to bookstores because the bookstore wholesalers take 55% discount—and that's more than your profit. So although you have less money tied up in inventory and low start-up costs, your per-book costs are too high to sell to bookstores or libraries. To be successful at POD publishing, you *must* plan to sell via a website or direct to consumers.

- Most POD publishers sell you your books at a 20-50% discount—which means (since their costs are substantially less than that) that they're making money on *your* book purchases, even if no one else buys the book.

- Some of the POD publishers make the book available to bookstores and other retail outlets. Usually this means that the book is listed in directories, and *if* anyone orders it, it is available to them. Few of the POD publishers do anything significant in terms of marketing, so it is unlikely that any will sell except through your direct efforts. Of course, this is also true of traditional (big) publishers in today's book climate.

- Most of the POD publishers (but again, not all) are not selective in the books they accept—because they're making money (on the up-front costs) whether or not you sell your book. This tends to lessen the overall perceived quality of their books (and indeed, of POD books in general.)

- Most POD books are ignored by reviewers.

- Most POD books are priced higher than similar titles

- Most POD titles are neither stocked in bookstores (because they're generally not returnable and bookstores require returns) nor sold to libraries (because they're overpriced, are offered at lower-than-standard discounts, and/or are of generally poor quality).

- POD is, at this time, most suitable for books that have little commercial value or for publishing houses with poor capitalization which may not be able to afford the printing costs of traditional small or self-publishing. Family histories or genealogies, family or community recipe books, poetry anthologies, and the like are good candidates for POD publishing. A recent article on POD in Writer's Digest Magazine revealed that the average POD author can expect to sell only a few dozen, perhaps a few hundred, books. Of course, as with all publishing maxims, there are occasional successes that beat the odds.

- In short, you may want to use a POD printer (first usage) to keep your initial cash outlay as small as possible, to avoid warehousing excess inventory, or to float a title that you are not sure will succeed. For the purposes of this book, such a use of POD just means that instead of using one of the offset printers, you will use a digital printer to print fewer books. A complete list of printers, including POD printers, is included on Day Number 24.

- If you are seriously interested in the other benefits a POD publisher (second usage) provides (such as cover and interior design and limited distribution) I suggest a careful examination of the following books and services which go into POD in the much greater detail that is beyond the scope of this book. I also recommend that you run the POD contract by an experienced publishing lawyer to make sure the terms are reasonable.

o Julie Duffy's *21ˢᵗ Century Publishing: An Author's Introduction to Print On-Demand Book Publishing.* This e-book is available from the author's site at www.JulieDuffy.com/ebook.

o Penny Sansevieri's *No More Rejections...Get Published Today!* This 260-page book compares all the POD vendors and is available at www.BooksByPen.com.

o John Harnish's *Everything You Always Wanted to Know About POD Publishing But Didn't Know Who To Ask.* This 600-pager was authored by a POD company staffer, and is available at www.BuyBooksOnTheWeb.com.

o Writers Collective is the only nonexclusive POD publisher offering authors 100% royalties and minimal (under $200) set up fees for services including customizable color covers, printing, and discounted distributor rates. Find out more information from Lisa Grant at www.WritersCollective.org.

o One final resource is Dehanna Bailee's online POD database, which lists over 35 POD publishers and compares their prices and offerings, including royalties, distribution, whether they provide an ISBN and barcode, and who does the cover and interior design. www.Geocities.com/dehannabailee/pod.htm

Exclusive Distributors

Next, decide whether you want an exclusive distributor.

- If you have an exclusive distributor, you can ignore the rest of today's tasks—you won't have to worry about non-exclusive distributors, wholesalers, or fulfillment houses. Exclusive distributors take much of the headache—and a good chunk of the profit—out of independent publishing.

- If you can get an exclusive distributor—many publishers can't—they will take exclusive control of your books. They will be responsible for working with all the wholesalers, other distributors, bookstores, and libraries—not only will you not need to interact with anyone else in the book trade, you won't be able to legally. They will take your books directly from the printer, and distribute them to where they are going. Most exclusive distributors will also demand their hefty percentage of your online sales, including Amazon.

- In return for these services—which often include the use of a sales force to present your book to the chain stores, and inclusion of your book in their catalogues and at book shows—they take at least 65-70% of your sales. (Like wholesalers, they'll pay in 90 days, and like wholesalers, they want full returns.)

- Some publishers feel that the advantage of an exclusive distributor is their ease in getting your books into bookstores. (I feel that as long as they're allowed returns, you might regret this ease—and prefer to do your own, non-returnable, distribution. Even if you're giving

returns, you might prefer to do your own distribution—
so that you can control the speed, and quantities, at which
your books are distributed, to minimize the potential
returns situation.)

- Independent publishers are in violent disagreement about
  whether the advantages of exclusive distribution
  outweigh the disadvantages. If you want to pursue
  exclusive distribution, send information on your title,
  including your marketing plans, to the following exclusive
  distributors:

  o Publishers Group West, 1700 4th Street, Berkeley, CA
    94710, (800)788-3123, fax (510)528-3444, info@
    pgw.com, www.pgw.com

  o Independent Publishers Group, 814 North Franklin
    Street, Chicago, IL 60610, (312)337-0747, fax
    (312)337-5985, frontdesk@ipgbook.com, www.
    ipgbook.com

  o Partners Book Distributing, 2325 Jarco Drive, Holt,
    MI 48842, (517)694-3205, fax (517)694-0617,
    PartnersBk@aol.com, (no web site)

  o Biblio, 4720 Boston Way, Lanham, MD 20706,
    (301)459-3366, fax (301)459-1705, www.biblio
    distribution.com

  o Consortium, 1045 Westgate Drive #90, St. Paul, MN
    55114, (800)283-3572, Consortium@cbsd.com, www.
    cbsd.com

- o Midpoint Trade Books, 1263 Southwest Blvd., Kansas City, KS 66103, (913)831-2233, fax (913)362-7401, Info@MidPt.com, www.MidPointTrade.com

- o National Book Network, 4720 Boston Way, Lanham, MD 20706, (301)459-3366, fax (301)459-1705, www.NBNBooks.com

- If you're certain you want an exclusive distributor, and are having difficulty getting one, Publishers Marketing Association has a program for members that may help. Submit your title to the PMA Trade Distribution Program for a $55 entry fee. Your title will be evaluated by a panel including buyers from Barnes & Noble, Waldenbooks, Baker & Taylor, Ingram, and Independent Publishers Group (a distributor). If your title is suitable, you'll be offered a standard exclusive distributorship through IPG. Send $55 and your book to: PMA, 627 Aviation Way, Manhattan Beach, CA 90266, or call (310)372-2732 for more details.

Distributor Bankruptcies

In the last few years, several distributors have gone belly up, taking the inventory from many small publishers with them. (If your distributor is in possession of your books on consignment, other creditors of the distributor can claim it.) So don't be so excited at the thought of getting a distributor that you neglect to think about what will happen if that distributor goes bankrupt: Give it some thought *before* you sign the agreement. Here are some things to consider before signing up with a distributor:

- Check their financial standing. Don't climb into bed with a company that's not doing well financially—if they go under, they may well take your books with them.

  Dun & Bradstreet is one company that will rate financial soundness; they offer a variety of reports, the least expensive of which is about $100. www.DNB.com

- Get references from current clients. (Ask the distributor for references, but also post to publishing lists and ask others.) Find out if other publishers are being paid on time consistently by them. Inconsistent, late, or irregular payments can be some of the early warning signs that a company is in trouble.

- Ask the distributor if you can warehouse your inventory privately, and ship your distributor only what they need to fulfill orders. This means more hassle for you, but if the distributor goes bankrupt, very few of your books will be at risk. (The distributor might be happy to acquiesce to this arrangement—it saves them the cost of warehousing your books.) Be sure you choose a warehouse that's dry, fireproof, and insured: Inspect the space and ask local fire authorities if it's suitable. A warehouse used to working with publishers is best.

- Ask if the distributor will sign a statement saying that, in the event of their bankruptcy, you are immediately free to contract to pursue sales through another distributor. This will allow you to ship books despite their bankruptcy— otherwise you might lose months, even years, waiting for your legal release. (Don't attempt this one on your own—find a good lawyer to draft this agreement.)

- Be sure your distribution agreement includes a clause stating that, despite who possesses your books, you own your inventory until the distributor sells (and pays you for) the books.

- Be sure your distributor signs a UCC-1 (Uniform Commercial Code-1) and that you file it with the county clerk of the town in which your distributor stores your books. (This is a legalism that gives you, as the consignee, first rights to your inventory.) You can get the UCC-1 form from any lawyer.

- Run *any* distribution agreement past a publishing attorney skilled in bankruptcy: Preventative medicine is always cheapest.

- Keep very careful track of invoices and payments, and have your accountant read the distributor's financial reports annually. If your distributor begins paying late or not at all, you may have a problem. Cease shipments to them until their payments are current.

- If, despite your best efforts, you end up selecting a distributor who goes bankrupt, here's what to do:

  o Get a bankruptcy lawyer. Do not try to navigate these waters yourself.

  o Try to reclaim your inventory. If you followed the earlier suggestion, you're warehousing your books privately, and don't have much tied up in your distributor's warehouse.

o   Contract with a new distributor as quickly as possible and let your major buyers and wholesalers know how to get your books. (If you've signed the earlier agreement that releases you from the agreement in the event of bankruptcy, you'll find this a lot easier.)

o   Realize that you're probably going to end up eating some of the returns—since the out-of-business distributor won't honor them, and your new distributor probably won't be ecstatic about taking on someone else's problem.

o   Most of all, don't despair! You will extract yourself from this mess in time, and go on to continue selling books.

Non-Exclusive Distributors

If you don't want an exclusive distributor—or you can't get one—consider a non-exclusive distributor. (If you're going to sign up with one or more non-exclusive distributors, you should *also* sign up with one or both wholesalers (see following section.)

• Non-exclusive distributors are smaller versions of wholesalers, with very similar terms: 55% discounts, books are returnable, payment in 90-120 days, you pay shipping.

• Unlike exclusive distributors, you may use the services of as many non-exclusive distributors as you like. (You may also use a combination of non-exclusive distributors and wholesalers.)

- Some people claim that they sell more books by listing with non-exclusive distributors—but I believe that as long as you're listed with both of the major wholesalers, Ingram and Baker & Taylor, you will make most of these sales anyway. It's unclear whether forming arrangements with these companies is worth the time and energy you'll put in. You'll need to submit a formal application of your book and publishing house to all these companies. Non-exclusive distributors include:

  o BookPeople, 7900 Edgewater Drive, Oakland, CA 94621, (510)632-4700, www.BPOnline.com

  o New Leaf, 401 Thornton Road, Lithia Springs, GA 30122, (770)948-7845, fax (770)944-2313, www.New LeafVendors.com

Library Distributors

Whether or not you have signed on with one or more non-exclusive distributors, consider a library distributor. The two major library distributors are also non-exclusive. Of the two, Quality Books has a bigger sales force and will sell more books for you; Unique is smaller and less effective. Both take 55%, buy returnable, and pay in 90-120 days. Again, you'll need to formally submit your book for consideration:

- Quality Books, Carolyn Olson, 1003 West Pines Road, Oregon, IL   61061, (815)732-4450, fax (815)732-4499, Carolyn.Olson@Quality-Books.com,   www.Quality -Books.com

- Unique Books, 5010 Kemper Avenue, St. Louis, MO 63139, (314)776-6695, fax (314)776-0841, UniqueBks@ aol.com, www.UniqueBooksInc.com

Library Wholesalers

Send your terms to library wholesalers. Unless you're working with an exclusive distributor, you should definitely send your terms and titles to the library wholesalers. Library wholesalers simply special order for libraries, and save you from losing potential library sales. In particular, do not neglect sending terms to Emery Pratt: Bowker just announced that library customers of BooksinPrint.com can now order directly online from Emery Pratt. Here's where to send your terms:

- The Book House, Inc., 208 W. Chicago Street, Jonesville, MI 49250, (517)849-2117, fax (517)849-4060, Bhinfo@ TheBookHouse.com

- Brodart, 500 Arch Street, Williamsport, PA 17705, (800)233-8467. bookinfo@brodart.com, www. brodart.com

- Emery Pratt, 1966 W. Main Street, Owosso, MI 48867, (517)723-5291, fax (517)723-4677, customer.service@ emery-pratt.com, www.emery-pratt.com

- Midwest Library Service, 11443 St. Charles Rock Road, Bridgeton, MO 63044, (314)739-3100, mail@midwestls .com, www.midwestls.com

- Academic Book Center, 5600 NE Hassalo Street, Portland, OR 97213, (503)287-6657, fax (503)284-8859, info@acbc.com, www.acbc.com

Independent Sales Representatives

Consider independent sales representation. If you think you'd like the help of a sales force, but are not interested in all the strings attached to using an exclusive distributor, consider hiring a sales representative on your own. You can find out more from The National Association of Independent Publishers Representatives, PMB 157, 111 East 14th Street, New York, NY 10003, (508)877-5328, fax (508)788-0208, NAIPR@aol.com, www.NAIPR.com.

Wholesalers

Get a wholesaler. If you're not going to have exclusive distribution, be sure to sign up with one or both of the major wholesalers. (You can—and should—sign up with wholesalers *and* non-exclusive distributors.)

- Ingram Book Company is the largest wholesaler in the country, and fills bookstore orders. Baker & Taylor is the second largest wholesaler, and fills some bookstore and many library orders.

- Neither does book publicity or promotion per se (though both offer mailings, advertisements, newsletter placements, and the like, all for fees) and until recently, neither did any distribution. Baker & Taylor just announced that it will be starting a distribution component as well, aimed mostly at $1 million plus independent publishers.

- Both wholesalers request 55% discounts (that means they pay you 45% of list price), returnable terms, free freight in both directions (orders and returns), 90-day credit terms, and are not exclusive—all of which, though they hate to tell you this, is negotiable.

- Ingram charges a one-time, new title listing fee of $50 per title. Baker & Taylor charges a one-time $125 set-up fee. (SPAN members can have this fee waived, but only if you are willing to accept standard B&T terms: 55% discount, returnability, and you pay shipping.)

- Sign up with these wholesalers as quickly as possible when launching your book campaign—it is extremely difficult to do ongoing sales to libraries and bookstores without them. Send them an announcement of your new title, the list of forthcoming titles you compiled on Day Number Eight and a complete marketing plan for how you'll be publicizing your book. Baker & Taylor will enter you into their system automatically as soon as they get a bookstore or library order for your title. Ingram no longer likes to deal with small presses, but if you send them a long list of forthcoming titles and a well-thought out marketing plan, you can still break into their system.

  o **Ingram:** Publisher Relations Department, Ingram Distribution Group, One Ingram Boulevard, La Vergne, TN 37086, (615)287-5350 or (800)937-8222 x5250, www.ingrambookgroup.com

- o **Baker & Taylor,** 44 Kirby Avenue, PO Box 734, Somerville, NJ 08876, (908)218-3803, fax (908)704-9460, www.btol.com Once you are listed with B&T, check periodically to make sure that your books are listed correctly; if not, email datafix@btol.com to have the details fixed.

- Another option is to make your books available to bookstores and libraries via a growing online wholesale option. At IndyBook you can buy a listing for $25/year plus a credit card processing fee of 5-12% depending on volume. Contact Bonnie Hayskar at info@IndyBook.com.

Online Bookstores

Unless you're going to work with an exclusive distributor—in which case they will handle your online bookstore sales—be sure you also sign up with the online bookstores.

- The online bookstores generally request the same terms as the wholesalers—55% discount, you pay shipping in both directions, and ability to return books.

- Unlike your arrangements with wholesalers and distributors, which can take several weeks or months, listing your book in the online bookstores is fairly quick. For that reason, you don't want to list your book until you have received your reviews from whichever of the review journals you are anticipating mentions—because once you are listed in the online bookstores, you will not receive any more journal reviews; they will consider your book already published, and decline to review it. See Day

Number 28 for more information on how to list your book with these online bookstores.

Fulfillment Houses

If you don't want to process, pack, and ship orders yourself, use a fulfillment house. Many fulfillment houses will take orders for you on their toll-free numbers, process them, and ship them. Some just handle the warehousing and shipping, and leave the order-taking up to you.

- Typical fees that fulfillment houses charge include:

  o Order processing

    ▪ There is usually a charge per order, and a charge per item (e.g. $2.00/order plus $0.35 per item).

    ▪ Some fulfillment houses charge different rates for retail orders (individual orders) versus bulk orders (from your wholesalers.)

    ▪ There are often minimums to meet each month.

    ▪ There may also be charges for using their shopping cart (if you let them handle your web orders).

    ▪ They may charge separately for phone orders, including per-call charges, and long-distance costs (if you have them answer your 800 number).

o Storage charges: Fulfillment houses typically either charge for storage, or set minimum order volumes that must be met. Typical charges are 1-2¢ per book per month.

o Returns: Fulfillment houses charge for handling returns (from retail customers and wholesalers). Typically the return charges are the same as those for outbound shipments.

o Setup fees: Most fulfillment houses charge some kind of setup fee, which can vary widely depending on the house and the services you will be using. These typically range from $100 to $350.

o Some fulfillment houses do not charge all of these separate fees, and instead charge a "flat-fee", usually as a percentage of net sales. Typical flat fees range from 10% to 35% of the retail price of your book, and depend on volume (the more books you sell, the less it costs you per book.)

Some fulfillment houses provide the ability to check your inventory, place special orders, and track customer shipments from their websites.

• Here are a few fulfillment houses that work successfully with independent publishers:

o Rayve Productions, PO Box 726, Windsor, CA 95492, (707)838-6200, fax (707)838-2220, RayvePro @aol.com, www.RayveProductions.com

o The Intrepid Group, 1331 Red Cedar Circle, Fort Collins, CO 80524, (970)493-3793, fax (970)493-8781, MediaDirector@IntrepidGroup.com o Book Clearing House, 46 Purdy Street, Harrison, NY 10528, (800)431-1579, fax (914)853-0398, www. BookCH.com

o Publishers Storage and Shipping, 46 Development Road, Fitchburg, MA 01420, (978)345-2121; fax (978)348-1233, www.pssc.com

o BookMasters, 2541 Ashland Road, Mansfield, OH 44905, (800)537-6727, fax (419)589-4040, www.Book Masters.com

o Publishers Pick & Pack, PO Box 4316, Danbury, CT 06813, (888)742-5554, PickPack@BookOrder Express.com

o Pathway Book Service, 4 White Brook Road, Gilsum, NH 03448, (800)345-6665, fax (603)357-2073, www.PathwayBook.com. Pathway offers flat-fee rates.

o PSI Fulfillment, 8803 Tara Lane, Austin, TX 78737, (800)460-0500, fax (512)288-5055, www.PSI Fulfillment.com

o Shipping-and-Handling.com, 5150 Palm Valley Rd #402 Ponte Vedra, FL 32082, (904)247-2016, fax (904)273-8448, admin@shipping-and-handling .com, www.shipping-and-handling.com

Do It All Yourself

The final option is to do all the distribution and fulfillment yourself: Here's how:

<u>Telephones</u>

- Get an 800 number. (People don't like paying for phone calls when ordering products.) So make it easy for them to order from you:

    o Available toll-free prefixes include 800, 888, 877, and 866. The best—if you can get one—is still 800, as it's recognized by the most people. Try `https://businessesales.att.com/products_services/tollfreeproduct_cataloglookup.jhtml` to see if the number you want is available.

    o Unfortunately, memorable numbers in the 800 series are almost all already in use. It's nice to have a memorable number—particularly if you're planning to do a lot of radio publicity, so that commuters remember your number once they're home and able to write it down! To find a good ("vanity") 800 number, you may need to use a consultant specializing in finding 800 numbers. One place to look for such consultants is `dir.yahoo.com/Business_and_Economy/Business_to_Business/Communications_and_Networking/Telecommunications/Phone_Services/1_800_Service/`.

- Once you have acquired your 800 number, or if you don't care what toll-free number you get, zero-in on the best and least expensive toll-free number provider. The following offer pricing comparisons:

    o `www.tollchaser.com/compare/tollfree/longdistancerates`

o www.BuyerZone.com (They offer a good buyer's guide, though their rate examples are somewhat out of date.)

o Qwest offers competitively priced long distance and toll-free service. www.Qwest.com

Note that the single rate they quote (e.g. 4.9¢) is a long-distance (*inter*-state) rate; the rates for calls to your 800 number from *within* your state (*intra*-state) rates usually differ by state—see their intra-state call rate tables. Be sure to look at plan details that can greatly affect your bottom line price, including:

o Minimum call length—you will be billed for this length of time for even the shortest call

o Billing increment—e.g. a billing increment of 6 seconds means that if you talk for 7 seconds, you get billed for 12 seconds [if there is no minimum length for a call]

o Monthly 800-number fee—Some plans charge a small fee per month for each 800 number you have

• Once you have an 800 order line, you have three choices:

o You can answer it yourself.

▪ If you're not going to be there around the clock, get an answering machine or voicemail, at least for your off-hours. If you're on the east coast, you can bet that the Californians will be calling after you've gone for dinner—and will be annoyed that there's no one to take their order.

- Make sure you call your number yourself and check for the following:

    ◆ Does the machine answer quickly enough? (You may need to set it so that it picks up after fewer rings.)

    ◆ Is the audio quality clear?

    ◆ Do you sound enthusiastic and professional?

    ◆ Is your message too long?

- If your telephone voice isn't attractive, consider hiring someone to tape your message: It's very inexpensive, and can result in many more orders. Try: Susan Berkeley, The Great Voice Company, 616 E. Palisade Avenue, Englewood Cliffs, NJ 07632, (201)541-8595, fax (201)541-8608, Susan@GreatVoice.com, www.GreatVoiceCo.com

○ Get an answering service. They'll answer your phone around the clock, and tell callers whatever you want. Unfortunately, great answering services are difficult to find. Here are a few that we've learned of; please let us know if you know of a great service!

    - PATLive offers a toll-free number and call answering service that operates according to scripts you provide them—they can take orders, etc. PATLive, 2024 North Point Boulevard, Tallahassee, FL 32308, (800)775-7790, fax (800)800-6126, www.PatLive.com

- Mountain West Communications, Hotchkiss, Colorado. Offers 24-hour service with orders transmitted via email or mail. Mountain West Communications, 110 E. Hotchkiss Ave., PO Box 216, Hotchkiss, CO 81419, (800)642-9378, fax (800)642-9378, www.mountwest .com

- Books Now. Offers 24/7 order taking plus 2-3 minute telephone recorded book previews. (800)BooksNow, www.BooksNow.com

- Telelink, a Canadian company, handles both the USA and Canada. Offers 24-hour service for $50/set up fee, $250 monthly minimum, .75/minute per incoming call. The Call Centre Inc., 2451 Cumberland Parkway, Suite 3225 Atlanta, GA 30339, (770)652-9909, fax (770)234-4255, www.TheCallCenterInc.com

- Anserphone uses a voicemail system with customized messages. The customer hears a pitch for your book, then speaks to a live operator. A much cheaper service than most. The Anserphone System, 3925 North I-10 Service Road West, Metairie, LA 70002, (800)872-8004, fax (504)867-1550, Info@ anserphone.com

- Answering Service Professionals charge a monthly price based on the number of phone calls you receive. Prices range from $82 per month for 110 phone calls to $310 per month for 525 phone calls. 154 Franklin Street, Valparaiso, IN 46383, (800)700-9798, fax (219)465-1075, asp@ring ading.com o Sign up with an order-taking service. Here is one:

- Book Clearing House (which also offers full fulfillment) offers its order line as an a la carte option, for 25% of retail price of the book. You can use their 800 number, or have them take calls from yours. (I recommend retaining your own 800 number.) You can also utilize their email and website for the same fee schedule. Customers pay them with credit cards, and they send you a monthly check (minus their 25%.) Contact Nancy Smoller, 46 Purdy Street, Harrison, NY 10528, (914)835-0015, fax (914)835-0398, BookCH@aol.com, www.BookCH.com

<u>Websites</u>

Set up a website for order-taking. This will also serve as your on-line storefront, information kiosk, and publicity opportunity.

- There are many, many details involved in establishing a website complete with book ordering capabilities (merchant account service and online shopping cart.) To understand the subject better I recommend reading one of the many excellent books on online business. Or check out the following sites online:

  o www.Ecommerce-Guide.com
    Contains overview of steps needed to set up an on-line business, as well as reviews of e-commerce software like shopping carts.

o   www.UseIt.com
     Website usability information

o   www.ECommerceTimes.com
     On-line e-business news

- If you want to take book orders online, you'll probably want a merchant credit account so that you can take credit cards. (You probably won't need an actual credit card machine, since you can enter orders online. You can still take credit cards at talks and workshops, just by having customers write their credit card numbers on the back of their business cards and processing them when you return home.) To do this, you need both a bank or merchant account provider that will let you accept credit cards, as well as the technological ability to process those credit cards. When shopping for a merchant account, keep in mind the following fees:

  o   Initial fees. Many banks charge for the initial set-up costs, including whatever equipment or software you will need to process transactions.

  o   Monthly fees. Most banks charge a flat monthly fee to service the merchant account, whether or not you have any transactions. Some charge fees only if you fall below a minimum transaction total.

  o   Transaction fees. Most banks also charge a fixed fee for every transaction. These fees can add up!

  o   Percentage fees. Most banks also charge a percentage of every sale, up to 3% or higher.

  o   Charge-back fees.

- A complete list of merchant account providers can be found at www.MerchantWorkz.com. Start here for comparisons of rates and services.

- Both American Express and Discover/Novus accept merchant account applications directly. These can be set up to process transactions from MasterCard and Visa, as well. Apply to:

  o www.AmericanExpress.com

  o www.DiscoverBiz.com

- Other merchant account providers:

  o Your local bank. Often, your local bank can give you a better rate than anyone.

  o PayPal. www.PayPal.com

  o Novus. www.NovusNetwork.com

  o ProPay. $35 set up fee, 3.5% plus $ .35 per transaction. No monthly minimums. (With ProPay, your charges will appear under your email address name rather than your business name—so be sure you have a business name that is also your email address.) www.ProPay.com

  o SPAN members can get merchant accounts easily through Electronic Transfer, Inc. Contact Mike Knudtson at (800)757-5453 x201.

  o PMA members can be set up with credit card capabilities through First National Bank. $50 set up fee, $7.50 per month. You must make a three-year commitment.

o Costco (you have to be a member.) Click on the Business tab, then Services, then look for Merchant Accounts.

o Quickbooks. Offers merchant services through Wells Fargo and Chase for $25 set-up fee, 2.35% plus $ .20 per transaction, and $11-15 per month. `http://merchantaccount.quickbooks.com/fee sQB.htm`

o Electronic Clearing House (Echo) $95 set up fee, 2.4% plus $ .15 per transaction plus $20 per month. (800)233-0406 x5. `wwws.echo-inc.com/`

- Once you have a merchant account set up, you need to select a shopping cart service to actually process your orders. Here are some considerations in selecting a shopping cart plan:

  o Be sure your shopping cart can calculate shipping, and charge appropriately for both priority and surface mail. If you're planning to accept foreign orders, be sure it can do that, too.

  o Be sure the service you choose can communicate with your accounting program so that you can download your list of customers easily, etc.

  o Choose a portable shopping cart, *not* one that is offered only by your web hosting company. You want to be able to change web-hosting companies with a minimum of hassle, if necessary; using your web host's shopping cart service will make it all that much more difficult to shift web hosts.

o Your merchant account provider may work directly with certain internet payment gateways, which in turn work with certain shopping carts. Make sure all three work together.

o The best shopping carts allow you to automate the entire process, so that you don't have to do any processing manually.

o Look at the reviews in www.Ecommerce-Guide.com.

- One company worth considering, because it is free of charge, is Mal's Shopping Cart, Mount Pleasant Cottage, Fairford, GLOS, GL7-4BA, United Kingdom. www.Mals-e.com

- ClickBank (only usable if you have an online merchant account). ClickBank.com

- QuikStore. www.QuikStore.com

- 1ShoppingCart.com, for $200-$600 annually. (888)255-6230, www.1ShoppingCart.com

- Be sure you apply for a secure encryption connection ("SSL") from your hosting company, so that your customers' credit card orders can't be hacked into and stolen. All web hosts offer this, but price and details vary.

- Most e-commerce service providers offer pre-packaged solutions that include shopping carts, merchant accounts internet payment gateways, web hosting, and more. If you don't want the hassle of configuring your own, try a prepackaged solution. Investigate the following:

o www.store.yahoo.com

o www.amazon.com Z Shops

- Make sure your website and 800 order number are listed on all your publications—stationery, letterhead, etc.

Order Fulfillment

- Put procedures in place so that order fulfillment (that means the process of shipping the books) will be smooth and flawless.

  o Make sure you establish foolproof procedures that will prevent you from losing orders. This will be different for every ordering system (e-mail, electronic, phone, etc.). For example, don't mark orders as shipped until they really have been shipped.

  o Make sure you pack the right book(s). Keep an outgoing inventory with the order until the package is sealed, and check every step of the way.

  o This is a good time to include other promotional material, such as announcements of your talks and workshops, catalogs, sale flyers, and postcards marketing your other books and products.

  o Send customers a confirmation email when they order and another when you ship the book.

o Make sure you've got customer service phone numbers and/or e-mail addresses on your web site and order forms, and respond quickly when customers contact you. The better your customer service, the better your business.

See Organize Your Shipping Department in Week Six for more information.

Make a Progress Chart

Now, put a big piece of graph paper on your wall. Put the upcoming weeks (for at least six months) along the bottom of the graph; put the quantities of books, in 25 book increments, along the left side. Every time you make a book sale, add it to the previous books sold and mark the total on your graph. This works as encouragement to dieters and budgeters—so why not for book sellers? As the numbers of books flying out of the garage increases, you'll be more and more motivated to sell more books—and the process will take on a life of its own.

This week you:

- Chose financial software
- Chose a company name
- Set up your legal structure
- Learned about the legalities
- Established your company
- Got an ISBN
- Filled out an ABI
- Set a discount schedule and terms
- Planned your future titles
- Established your website
- Decided how to sell your books
- Considered Print on Demand

Congratulations! Your book is on its way!

Week Number Three

☞ ☜

This week you'll:

- Create a support network

- Order a barcode

- Send for a copyright form

- Finalize your cover copy

- Zero-in on a cover designer

- Plan your cover art

Day Number 11

Today you'll **create a support network**.

Create a Support Network

Successful publishers—like all successful entrepreneurs— have support networks. Even loners need support, particularly with a job that requires long hours of alone time at your computer. A supportive group of business advisors will not just counter loneliness; they will be a valuable business asset. A professional network will provide you with advice, ideas, and connections, as well as expertise that would be difficult, if not impossible, to replicate on your own. Creating such a network is definitely worth your time. Here's how to create your own network:

• First, find a professional or peer network. Your best advice will come from other publishers. So make an effort to meet them!

   o Go to professional conferences, such as those organized by Publishers Marketing Association and SPAN.

      ▪ Publishers Marketing Association, 627 Aviation Way, Manhattan Beach, CA 90266, (310)372-2732, fax (310)374-3342, PMAonline@aol.com, www.PMA-online.org

- SPAN (Small Publishers of North America), PO Box 1306, Buena Vista, CO 80211, (719)395-4790, fax (719)395-8374, Span@Spannet.org, www.Spannet.org

o Join online discussions where publishers participate. Publishers are friendly folk and share advice freely; one day you'll be asking the questions, the next day you'll be able to help someone else by answering them. Here are a few of the best publishing lists:

- PUB-L. Send email to ListServ@ShrSys.HSLC.org with the words *Subscribe Publish-L* in the body (not the subject line) of the message.

- SPAN. Send email to Self-Publishing-Subscribe@Yahoogroups.com

- Pub-forum. Send email to majordomo @majordomo.alentus.com with the words *subscribe pub-forum you@youremail.com* in the *body* (not the subject line) of the message.

- About.Publishing. Go to www.Publishing.About.com

- Independent Publisher Online. Go to www.IndependentPublisher.com, or send email to JimB@BookPublishing.com

- Alt.Publish. Go to www.groups.google.com and search for *alt.publish.books.*

- Indy_Publishers. Send email to Indy_Publishers-subscribe@Yahoogroups.com o Check out the extremely helpful sites of publishing professionals, some of whom have compiled information to help market their books or services, others of whom have done it purely to be helpful. I highly recommend the following:

- John Kremer's site has a wealth of useful information. www.BookMarket.com

- Dan Poynter's site is the ultimate for self-publishers. Check it out at www.ParaPub.com.

- Graphic designer Pete Masterson has compiled an impressive list of printers and production and design tips. www.Aeonix.com.

- Jim Cox of Midwest Book Review has tips and links at www.MidwestBookReview.com.

- Pat Bell's Tool Shed contains all sorts of information on self-publishing, including (sometimes outdated) lists of vendors. www.CatsPawPress.com

- BookZonePro. Check out the valuable links under "Web Resources" at www.BookZonePro.com.

• Second, don't forget to enlist the services of a publishing lawyer and tax preparer when you're creating your network of supporters. See the earlier section on publishing lawyers.

• Technical advisors. You will probably need to hire all sorts of different people for particular projects (cover design, interior design, editing, web design) or short-term advice or assistance (publicity, advertising, etc.) These details are covered in greater depth in the chapter in which they appear. However, here are some generalities to remember in subcontracting for particular projects or jobs:

o   Remember to ask professional associates, including online friends, for recommendations. While I've included information throughout this book on my favorite experts, the best way to find referrals is by asking the people who do things similar to what you do. If you're publishing children's books, ask children's book publishers for their recommendations in cover designers, editors, etc.

o   Interview your possibilities. Ask about their experience, their fees, and their availability. Ask how long the task will take. Ask how much back-and-forth there will be (some cover artists, for example, do two covers and you pick between them; others expect a longer interaction and back-and-forth.) Ask whether the first consult is free. Find out what extras aren't included in the price, and when the fees need to be paid. Ask what you'll be required to supply for them to do their job most efficiently. See whether you feel comfortable with the conversation, and whether you'd like to work with them.

•   Make sure you're in touch with business advisors. The U.S. Small Business Administration (SBA) assists small businesses with information and services. One of their best programs is their volunteer advisory service, SCORE (Service Corps of Retired Executives.) These retired business executives volunteer to share knowledge and experience with small business owners with similar business interests. SBA also offers inexpensive publications, consulting services, and a loan program, as well as online courses developed in conjunction with *Inc.* magazine and Harvard Business School. Contact SBA for details: (800)827-5722 or www.SBA.gov.

- Friends. I find it incredibly helpful to keep a list of publishing friends, whom I've conversed with online or off and now have a relationship with, to ask my tricky questions. Sometimes, it's not a technical question I have—like, who is the best printer?—but a question that requires more thought or a judgment call. Particularly if it's something proprietary that I'm not sure I'm ready to announce to the world (like a new experiment or venture I'm hatching) I may want to run it by my publishing friends to hear their take on it. Don't forget to thank them (it's not their job to help you!) and make sure you pay for the phone call if they're helping you.

- Family. Don't forget your family. All family members might not be as interested or invested in your publishing house as you are, but they're your family, so they get to listen anyway. And having a supportive family can make all the difference in launching a successful—or just mediocre—publishing venture. My husband, nine year old, five year old, and infant tag along with me to conferences, conventions, and speaking engagements, and are tremendously helpful both in emotional support— "You'll do great, Mommy!"—and in marketing support. At the last Book Expo, my children met, and sold books to more people than I did!

Day Number 12

Today, you'll get a **barcode** for your book and send for a **copyright** form.

Order a Barcode

Once you have your ISBN, your title, and your price, you can get a barcode for your book. Here's more:

- The barcode—much like a supermarket barcode—can be scanned to identify the title, author, publisher, edition (hard or softcover), and price. Here's what the numbers mean:

  o Above the barcode is printed the book's ISBN.

  o Below the barcode, there are three groups of digits. The first three numbers (978) mean that the product is a book. The following nine digits are the ISBN of the book. The last digit is the check digit.

  o On the smaller barcode to the right, the first digit signals type of currency ("5" is U.S. dollars.) The next four digits signal the retail price of the book.

- All wholesalers and bookstores require books they carry to have such a barcode. (If your book doesn't have one, they will probably sticker one on and charge you for that service.)

- The barcode specific to books is called the "Bookland EAN with price code extension." EAN stands for European Article Number, and is international product code standard. Price code extension simply means that the retail price of the book will be coded directly into the barcode for easier scanning.

- The barcode is printed on the lower half of the back cover of your book, right above or below the ISBN number.

- The barcode costs between $10 and $30 and is available from a variety of vendors: Bowker can send you an updated list of suppliers upon request, or you can find suppliers at www.isbn.org/standards/home/isbn/us/barcode.html. Here are just a few:

  o Bar Code Graphics, 875 N. Michigan Avenue, Chicago, IL 60611, (800)662-0701, fax (312)664-4939, www.Barcode-Graphics.com

  o Fotel Inc., 1125 E. St Charles Road, Lombard, IL 60148, (800)834-4920, fax (630)932-7610, www.Fotel.com

  o General Graphics, 1608 Leishman Avenue, Arnold, PA 15068, (800)887-5894, fax (724)337-6589, sales@ggbarcode.com, www.ggbarcode.com

  o J&D Barcodes, 1821 S. Myrtle Avenue, Monrovia, CA 91016, (800)456-2926, fax (626)303-5432

- o Precision Photography, 1150 North Tustin Avenue, Anaheim, CA 92807, (800)872-9977, fax (714)630-6581

- o PIPS, 436 East 87th Street, New York, NY 10128, (888)783-7439, fax (212)410-7795, www.Pips.com

- You can buy a barcode yourself. They'll send you the film for the back cover directly. The Book Industry Study Group offers a booklet on Machine Readable Coding Guidelines. See the website at www.bisg.org. You'll need to supply the vendor with the following information:

  o Book title

  o ISBN

  o Price of book in U.S. dollars

  o Hardcover or softcover

  o Size of barcode (most common is 2" by 1⅛")

  o Magnification (most common is 90%)

  o Whether you want film (positive or negative) or an .eps (encapsulated Postscript) electronic file

  o Remember to leave some space around the barcode.

  o Request a black barcode on white background so that it scans properly.

- You can also acquire software that lets you produce your own barcodes. Try the following companies:

  o Azalea Software, 219 1st Avenue S, Seattle, WA 98104, (800)482-7638, fax (206)341-9881, azalea@ igc.org, www.azalea.com

  o SNX, 692 10th Street, Brooklyn, NY 11215, (718)499-6293, www.SNX.com

  o Worth Data, 623 Swift Street, Santa Cruz, CA 95060, (800)345-4220, www.BarcodeHQ.com

- You can get a free(!) barcode at www.cgpp.com/ bookland/isbn.html.

- Or you can let your cover artist take care of this arrangement. Letting your cover designer handle it is preferable, because she'll know the exact dimensions and specifications she'll need.

- If you're going to sell your book in drugstores and grocery stores, you will also need the Price Point UPC (Universal Product Code) with ISBN Add On barcode. It costs $750, which gives you 99,999 bar code numbers— there's no way to buy fewer for less money. Most books won't need this, but if yours will, contact the Uniform Code Council, 7887 Washington Village Drive #300, Dayton, OH 45459, (937)435-3870, fax (937)435-7317, www.uccouncil.org.

Send for a Copyright Form

Today you'll also send for a copyright form (which you'll register after your books are printed.) Write to request Form TX from: Register of Copyrights, Library of Congress, Washington, DC 20559, (202)707-9100, `lcweb.loc.gov/copyright`.

Consider also registering your work with the Writers Guild of America's new intellectual property registration service. For only $20 ($10 if you're a WGA member) you can register your intellectual property (thus conveying some legal protection on a work before copyrighting it.) More details are available at the Writers Guild of America website at `www.wga.org/registration/register-online.html`.

Day Number 13

Today, you'll finalize your **cover copy**.

Finalize Your Cover Copy

On Day Number Three you began writing your cover copy. Today you'll finalize it.

- If a famous person has given you a great quote, definitely put her name on your cover. (If she's particularly famous, put it on the front cover.)

- If you have *not* gotten an endorsement from someone famous, write your own best quote and stick it on the back cover without attribution.

- Include the ISBN and retail price of the book. (Bookstores will sticker it on anyway, and then you'll always to be trying to scrape the sticky off the returned books.) If you're planning extensive marketing in Canada, also include a Canadian retail price.

- Remember to include one (or two or three, if appropriate) BISAC categories in the upper left hand corner of the back cover. Bookstores use these headings for shelving. You can buy a list of the current BISAC codes from the producer, the Book Industry Study Group, at www.BISG.org. If you're a PMA member, you can get the list at half-price through the PMA website (www.PMA-online.org.) Or you can just look at the headings on books in the bookstore that are similar to yours, and make an educated guess. (We can't include the list here because it is copyrighted, though it is available by searching online.)

- Be sure to include the name of your publishing house, city, state, and website.

- Include your publishing house logo, if you have one. (One good source of royalty-free art for a low price, if you'd like an inexpensive logo, is www.ArtToday.com)

- Don't make the back cover copy too long. If it looks too dense, people won't read it.

- Once your cover is done, get expert advice on whether it works.

  o John Kremer, author of *1001 Ways to Market Your Books* offers 10-minute cover critiques by telephone for $50. Contact John Kremer, Open Horizons, PO Box 205, Fairfield, IA 52556, (800)796-6130, fax (641)472-1560, JohnKremer@BookMarket.com

Day Number 14

Today, you'll zero-in on a **cover designer**.

Zero-in on a Cover Designer

The best way to find a cover designer is to find several books whose covers you adore, and track down the cover designer. That way, you not only know they do professional work, but can also tell them, "I'd like something similar to the cover you did for X book." Be sure you use a designer who specializes in *book* covers. Here are some cover designers that independent publishers have worked with.

- Mayapriya Long designed the cover for this book. You can reach her at BookWrights, 2255 Westover Drive #108, Charlottesville, VA 22901, (804)823-8223, www. BookWrights.com.

- Pete Masterson, Aeonix Publishing Group, PO Box 20985, El Sobrante, CA 94820, (510)222-6743, Pete@ Aeonix.com, www.Aeonix.com

- Barry Kerrigan, DeskTop Miracles, 112 South Main Street, Stowe, VT 05672. (802)253-7900, fax (802)253-1900, Barry@DeskTopMiracles.com, www.DeskTop Miracles.com

- Pamela Terry of Opus 1 Design, PO Box 3653, Beverly Hills, CA 90212, (800)590-7778, fax (323)934-2881, www.Opus1Design.com

- Lightbourne, 258 A Street #5, Ashland, OR   97520, (800)697-9833, fax (541)482-1730, www.Lightbourne .com

Day Number 15

Today you'll begin planning your **cover**. (You'll do this before you find an editor for your book, so that these two lengthy processes—the cover design, and the editing—will be completed roughly together.)

Plan Your Cover Art

There are many different approaches to planning a book cover. Some experts recommend starting by finding a good cover artist; others argue that you should start by writing the back cover copy. I recommend starting the cover as soon as possible—so that your cover artist can be doing her thing while the book is being edited. If you have the cover completed before you begin the interior design, you can also coordinate fonts, using the same font inside and out, so that the entire book looks like one cohesive package.

Whichever your approach, be sure to consider the following:

- Don't neglect the spine of the book. It's the first thing bookstore and library browsers will see—and if they don't like it, the only part of your book they will see! It should include the title, subtitle, author, and publisher of your book; some publishers also include a publishing house logo. (Once you have selected a printer and paper thickness, your cover artist will need to know the spine width of the book in order to finish the cover design. To calculate the spine width of your book, you'll divide the total number of pages by the PPI (pages per inch) of the text paper you will use and add in the thickness of the two covers. Since this changes according to the paper used, be sure to check with the printer.)

- Make sure that the cover design still looks good when it's shrunk down to postage-stamp size; that's the amount of space you have to convey an impression in online listings such as Amazon.

- Be sure the cover looks good when you see it in black and white. Most publications will display the cover in black and white, and you want it to still look striking, rather than gray.

- In general, avoid yellow and white covers. Yellow tends to fade, and white can show scuff marks easily.

- Make sure the title is the dominant visual image on the cover, and that it can be read easily from across the room.

  - Be sure your cover is in full color. Some beginning publishers think they'll save costs by printing a black and white or one-color cover—but that is foolish economy. Your cover is going to sell your book—make it the zippiest, liveliest cover you can! That means a 4-color—also known as CMYK—cover. (Four-Color process uses four translucent inks (cyan, magenta, yellow and black) that can be layered to create any color.)

- If you have any related books, consider adding their (front) cover art to the back cover of your book. (See the back cover of this book for an example.)

- Consider putting a small (professional!) photo of yourself on the back cover. If you're planning to do a lot of speaking, this is particularly worthwhile. (If you have a lot of other things to put on the back cover, move the photo inside; the back cover should be reserved for truly important items.)

- Because your back cover is such expensive real estate, if you have a bio that will really enhance sales, include it on the back. If your endorsements or reviews are better than your bio, consign the bio to the back of the book, on the page before your order form.

- Covers range in price, depending in part upon the professionalism and experience of the cover artist. You should be able to get a great cover for under $1,500.

- Once you have discussed the project, the cover artist will come up with one or more rough sketches. All cover artists work differently, but most are prepared to do some back-and-forth until you have something you're satisfied with.

- Be sure you own all rights to your cover. Sign a work-for-hire contract with your cover artist that allows you to use the cover for uses besides the book cover—for promotional purposes on postcards, flyers, t-shirts, websites, etc. Without such a legal contract, you may find yourself paying royalties to your cover designer for every use of the cover—whether or not you thought you owned it because you paid for it. Consult a good publishing lawyer for more information on how to draw up this contract.

This week you:

- **Created a support network**

- **Ordered a barcode**

- **Send for a copyright form**

- **Finalized your cover copy**

- **Zeroed-in on a cover designer**

- **Planned your cover art**

Congratulations! You're building momentum!

Week Number Four

Cʒ ʂ

Thix week you'll:

- Choose an editor

- Finalize your manuscript

- Send advance galleys to reviewers

- Send advance galleys to chain stores

- Request cataloging-in-publication data

Day Number 16

Today, you'll **choose an editor** for your book.

Choose an Editor

Even crackerjack writers require editing. A good editor can turn a ho-hum book into a good book, and a good book into a great book. More importantly, a good editor can fix up all the little spelling and grammatical errors that make your book look less than professional, and transform your writing into prose that's clear and understandable. (And the best spell-checker won't replace a good editor. "Eye kin rite awl write" is correctly spelled—but still wrong.) Good editing will make your book more appealing to reviewers, the media, and eventually, the public. Don't ignore this part, and don't downplay its importance; the best cover in the world won't compensate for clumsy, unclear writing: Hire an editor. Here's how:

- First, decide what type of editing your book requires. Copy editing is the least expensive, least rigorous form of editing. When you pay to have your book copy edited, the editor will fix up the spelling, the grammar, and the run-on sentences. More intensive editing, also called line editing, (which will be commensurately more expensive) will also include reorganizing the material for clarity. Decide how rigorous an editing job would benefit your book.

- Second, contact a few editors and tell them what you're looking for. Ask whether they've edited something similar. Good editors can edit anything, but even the best editors usually have areas that they're more or less comfortable editing.

- Explain your time constraints. Most editors work by the hour; some work by the project. If they quote you an hourly fee, ask how long they anticipate the job taking. Most good editors can estimate this fairly accurately, but consider asking for a cap or having them check back with you if it's taking longer than expected. Many editors do freelance work in between regular jobs, so make sure they'll be able to fit you in by your deadline.

- If your editor is doing a lot more than just copy editing for your book, be sure you sign a work-for-hire contract so that there's no question about ownership of your manuscript. Otherwise, you may find yourself paying royalties for years to come. Consult with a publishing lawyer for more information.

- There are hundreds, perhaps thousands, of freelance editors. Many have listings in publications such as *Literary Market Place*. You can also find quality editors through the Editorial Freelancers Association, www.the-efa.org. If you belong to a writing or publishing group or list, ask for recommendations. Or contact one of the top-notch editors below:

  o Sharon Goldinger, PeopleSpeak, 25342 Costeau, Laguna Hills, CA 92653, (949)581-6190, fax (949)581-4958, PplSpeak@Nayzak.com, www.

DetailsPlease.com/PeopleSpeak. Rates vary by project.

o Jeanette Leardi, 1716-2H Charleston Place Lane, Charlotte, NC 28212, (704)531-0787, jleardi@ mindspring.com. $35-45/hour for copy editing; $50+/hour for line editing.

o Diane Feldman, 550 Maple Avenue, Teaneck, NJ 07666, (973)251-5047, DianeF@Pennwell.com. $35/hour for copy editing.

o Laurie Kahn, 23-07 21st Street, Astoria, NY 11105, LexiKahn@att.net. $25/hour for copy editing; $50/hour for line editing.

Day Number 17

Today you'll **finalize your manuscript** in preparation for submission to reviewers and chain stores.

Finalize Your Manuscript

Today, before sending your book off to reviewers and chain store buyers (tomorrow's task), you'll finalize the manuscript. Here's what your advance galleys do—and do not—need to include:

- Include the bulk of the manuscript, so that reviewers can get a sense of what the finished book will look like.

- Don't worry about minor additions or corrections. If there is still data missing, just pencil the letters T/K into the manuscript, to indicate to reviewers that the information is en route, and that you know you've omitted it.

- Don't worry if the art isn't included. Just mark out in the manuscript where the art will go, and (roughly) of what it will consist.

- Don't worry about typographical errors, or minor grammatical or spelling errors. If there are too many it won't look professional, but no one expects this manuscript to be perfect—that's why it's called an advance galley.

- It's not necessary to include appendices (glossary, bibliography, index, author biography) in the advance galley. Just insert a placeholder showing where those elements will go if you plan to include them in the final version of the book.

- It's not necessary to include cataloging in publication data—you'll be applying for that shortly. Reviewers don't expect you to have this data for the advance copies (though it is important to note that it is pending, and that you will have it for the final version of the book.)

Day Number 18

Today, you'll send **advance galleys to reviewers.**

Send Advance Galleys to Reviewers

Advance galleys—sometimes called advance reading copies (ARCs); the terms are identical—are a not-quite-final, not completely polished, pre-production version of your book that is sent to key reviewers, preferably four to six months before publication date. The cover of the galley is generally uncoated and fairly empty (often with only the name of the book, publisher, and ISBN); the back with perhaps a synopsis, blurbs, and author info.

Sending these advance galleys out to reviewers is a crucial step. Without reviews from major journals, you are seriously limiting your sales to bookstores and particularly libraries, regardless of the quality of your book. If you can score a review in *BookList* or *Library Journal*, you automatically guarantee several thousand sales to libraries. The good news is that, with a good manuscript, reviews are fairly easy to get. Here are some issues to consider and things to do:

- Send your review copy immediately, because getting a review takes time. Most of the journals work at least three to six months in advance. Make sure you enclose a cover letter that tells the reviewer your publication date (which has nothing to do with the date your books are printed, and which you arbitrarily set to be whenever you want) and make sure the publication date is sufficiently far ahead—at least three to six months off—that the journals will have time to schedule the review of your book.

- Don't send galleys *just* to the eminent review journals listed here. (Almost everyone makes this mistake, which can make the difference between abysmal sales and fantastic sales!) While it is undeniably true that a great review in Publishers Weekly or Library Journal will guarantee thousands of sales to bookstores or libraries, you will often sell more books targeting your audience specifically. Figure out the audience for your book and send to *those* magazines and newspapers for review. A book on writing will sell more copies via a good review in Writer's Digest than Publishers Weekly; a book on cows will do better with Hoard's Dairyman than Library Journal. (Another consideration is that the more specialized publications will review even sub-optimal books that the larger journals wouldn't consider.)

- Many beginning publishers neglect sending review copies to library journals, because they are ambivalent about the idea of library sales: Why sell to one library, when you can sell to thousands of individuals? The answer is that good library sales actually lead to good individual sales— because people are quite likely to see your book in a library, even read the library copy, and then buy their own. (This is particularly true for a non-fiction nuts-and-bolts book.) And word of mouth is easier to get going if books are in libraries. Finally, library sales add up quickly—and can total 5,000 to 10,000 copies or more for a good subject done well. Don't pass up these guaranteed sales.

- This is what reviewers will be looking for in evaluating whether to review your book:

  o Does it meet basic book requirements? Does the book have an ISBN, and library cataloging data?

  o Will it be available to bookstores and libraries? Is there a distributor, or is the publishing house listed with Ingram or Baker & Taylor?

  o Does the book look nice? Is the font readable and appropriate? Does the interior design look professional?

  o Does it meet literary standards? Are there obvious typographical errors or grammatical mistakes?

  o If you've included a sample cover, is it professional? Is the title and author name professionally laid out? Is the publisher name on the book's spine? Is there a barcode? Is the price listed on the cover?

  o Does the author have credible credentials?

  o Has anyone credible or famous endorsed the text?

  o Is there an appropriate marketing plan for the book?

- Advance galleys have plain bindings and no finished cover. The reality of today's publishing is that it's sometimes easier to send finished books. However, major review journals insist on reviewing galleys, and won't review finished books. To get around the conundrum, you have two good choices: You can print up a few galleys, for the handful of reviewers who won't look at finished books, or you can mutilate finished books and pretend they're advance galleys (rip off the covers and replace with plain cardboard bindings). Your local copy shop can do either of these for you. The following companies produce advance galleys:

o Country Press, PO Box 489, Middleborough, MA 02346, (508)947-4485, fax (508)947-8989

o Crane Duplicating, 17 Shad Hole Road, Dennisport, MA 02369, (508)760-1601, www.CraneDuplicating.com

o DeHarts, 3265 Scott Boulevard, Santa Clara, CA 95054, (800)982-4763, fax (408)982-9912, www.DeHarts.com

o Fidlar Doubleday, 6255 Technology Avenue, Kalamazoo, MI 49009, (800)632-2259, fax (888)999-0655, www.Fidlar.com

o Quebecor World, 1989 Arcata Boulevard, Martinsburg, WV 25402, (304)267-3600, fax (304)267-0989, www.QuebecorWorld.com

o R. R. Donnelley, 77 W. Wacker Drive, Chicago, IL 60601, (312)326-8000, www.RRDonnelley.com

o Sterling Pierce, 422 Atlantic Avenue, East Rockaway, NY 11518, (561)593-1170, fax (516)593-1401

Or, simply bring your manuscript to the nearest Kinko's or similar copy shop for quick (but pricey) galleys.

- Here's the information you should type on the front cover of the galley:

  o The words "Uncorrected Proof" or "Advance Review Copy"

  o Title, subtitle, and author of the book

  o ISBN and BISAC categories (For example, this book's categories are Writing/Reference.)

  o Publisher name and contact information (address, telephone, website, email)

  o Publication month (again, make this up, and set it at least three to six months from now to maximize your publicity and reviews)

  o Retail price, page count, trim size (the dimensions of the book—5.5 by 8.5, for example), binding (softcover or hardcover), back matter if any (appendices, index, bibliography, or glossary; libraries, in particular, like to see books with plenty of back matter)

  o Distribution (Ingram, Baker & Taylor)

  o Library cataloging numbers (Just write "CIP pending")

  o Size of print run (only include this if you're going to tell them at least 30,000)

  o Author tour details. Only include if you're going to five cities or more.

- o Ad/promotion budget. Include only if more than $30,000.

- o Any advance quotes

- o Name of publicist who can be contacted for more details

- Along with the galley itself, send reviewers a cover letter. You can sign it with the name of a "publicist" if you like. The letter should include all the details above, as well as a description of the contents, why the book is important, who the market is, and the author's credentials, including previously published books.

- Be sure to mail all review copies priority mail or overnight.

- One caveat about reviews: Amazon now posts all reviews—Publishers Weekly, Library Journal, Kirkus, etc—at the very top of their listings, even above the book's basic description. That's great if you've garnered a fantastic review—and terrible if you have a lukewarm review. If you aren't positive your book will get a great review, and you anticipate heavy Amazon sales, it might be safer to avoid the entire review journal process, so you can write your own editorial copy for your Amazon listing instead of possibly being stuck with a mediocre review from one of the biggies.

- Send your books to the following reviewers:

- o *Publishers Weekly*, 245 West 17th Street, New York, NY 10011, (212)463-6782, fax (212)463-6631, www.

PublishersWeekly.reviewsnews.com/index.as
p?layout=submissions

Publishers Weekly reviews 5,000 books out of close to 50,000 submissions. Send galleys 3 months before publication date; they never review books after publication date. Their new submissions guidelines indicate that they *will* consider self-published books, if you "print at least 2,000 and have an arrangement with a reputable distributor." (But your chances of being reviewed are higher if you do not call yourself "self-published.")

o *Library Journal*, Book Review Editor, 245 West 17th Street, New York, NY 10011, Toll-free (888)800-5473   or   (212)463-6818,   fax   (212)463-6734, BkRev@LJ.Cahners.com,   www.libraryjournal .com/about/submission.asp

Library Journal goes to over 28,000 librarians: 50% of them public libraries, 21% academic libraries, 13% special libraries, and 6% school libraries. They review 6,000 books out of 40,000 submissions. A good review in Library Journal, according to their own promotional material, will sell over 1,000 books; a rave review on a high-demand topic may move 5,000. Most of these library orders will come through a library wholesaler, and some 80% of these through Baker & Taylor. Send galleys 3-4 months before publication date.

o American Library Association *Booklist* Magazine, 50 East Huron Street, Chicago, IL 60611, (800)545-2433, fax (312)337-6787, www.ala.org/booklist, or email Bonnie Smothers at BSmothers@ala.org or Editor and Publisher Bill Ott at Bott@ala.org.

Booklist reviews 4,000 adult books, 2,500 children's books, and 500 reference books each year. Send galleys 3-4 months before publication date.

- Adult books to Brad Hooper

- Children's books to Stephanie Zvirin

- Reference books to Mary Ellen Quinn

o *Foreword Magazine*, Alex Moore, Book Review Editor, 129½ East Front Street, Traverse City, MI 49684, (231)933-3699, fax (231)933-3899, www.Foreword Magazine.com/reviews/revsguidelines.asp

Foreword reviews books from independent and university presses. Submit galleys and cover art 3-4 months before publication date. They review 600 books (out of 7,000 submitted) each year, 90% of which are nonfiction. Circulation is 20,000.

o *Kirkus Reviews*, 770 Broadway, New York, NY 10003, (212)777-4554, fax (212)979-1352, www.Kirkus Reviews.com

Send Kirkus *two* copies of galleys at least 3 months before publication date. They receive over 70,000 manuscripts.

o *The New York Times Book Review*, 229 W. 43rd Street, New York, NY 10036, (212)556-7267 o   *School Library Journal,* 245 W. 17th Street, New York, NY 10011, (212)463-6759

   Send only books appropriate for K-12 school libraries.

- In addition to pursuing the biggest review journals, you might want to spend some time getting reviews from smaller publications. Reviews from groups respected by your niche market are much easier to come by than reviews in Publishers Weekly—and are more likely to sell books to readers in your niche. Check *The Encyclopedia of Associations, The Oxbridge Directory of Newsletters* and *Standard Rate and Data Services Business Publications* for outstanding lists of associations, varied newsletters, and trade publications respectively, for publications that might be interested in reviewing your book.

Day Number 19

Today, you'll send **advance galleys to chain stores**.

Send Advance Galleys to Chain Stores

Today you'll also send advance galleys to the major chain stores. (You'll follow up with a finished copy of the book as soon as you have books back from the printer, but it's best to approach the chains as early in the process as possible; they plan six months in advance.)

- The basic process for getting your book into the chains is to submit the advance galleys and your ABI form to the Small Press Department or New Vendor Acquisitions (depending on the chain). Those departments then evaluate your manuscript (using roughly the same criteria as the reviewers.) If it passes their initial screening, it gets passed on to the category buyer, who buys all the books that the chain carries in that particular area: Fiction, Children's, Health, etc.

- Based on experience, the buyer then makes a decision about whether to carry your book, and how many books, and in which stores, to carry it. (If they really like your book, they may decide to *model* it, which means that rather than letting it go out of stock, they will automatically replace every book that is sold with another order for the book.) Often, the buyer will start with a small order and see how the book does; sometimes they will order it for just a few stores and then expand to a greater range of stores if the book is successful. The more unique the title, the better your chances of being sold and modeled, but many factors influence whether the chains will buy your title.

- For example, my book, *The Infertility Diet: Get Pregnant and Prevent Miscarriage*, sells several thousand copies per year through Barnes and Noble, where it is modeled in several hundred stores, because there still are no competing titles offering a nutritional approach to infertility and miscarriage. My title, *Terrorism and Kids: Comforting Your Child*, although it was purchased and sold well through B&N, was never modeled, because B&N (correctly, I think) perceived it as a title of limited duration, that would stop selling once circumstances (hopefully) changed.

- Once your book is carried by the chains, attempt to make personal contact with the buyers if possible (but without pestering them.) PMA runs occasional "Meet the Buyers" days as part of their annual conference; don't miss this opportunity to get to know your buyer in person!

- One final word on working with the chains. Many new publishers ask me about buying endcaps (the end of aisle displays) and other in-store display space for their titles. Keep in mind that:

  o Buying in-store display space is probably an ineffective use of your marketing/advertising money—and you'd be better off spending it on more editorial coverage.

o The chain stores usually initiate such purchases themselves with titles they think would succeed in the spaces.

o The chains are *extremely* proprietary about their pricing for such in-store displays. You generally need to sign a non-disclosure agreement before they will tell you what these options cost.

o There are small press discounts for in-store displays (Barnes & Noble, for example, offers everything at half price for small presses) but since there's no easy way to ask other publishers what they've been charged (because of the non-disclosure agreements) it's still difficult to figure out if you're getting a "good deal" on such displays. B&N claims that they'll work with small presses to come up with pricing that is affordable.

o Do keep in mind that, as with advertising in general, bargaining is allowed, even encouraged.

• Here's where to send your advance copies:

o Marcella Smith, Barnes & Noble Small Press Department, 122 Fifth Avenue, New York, NY 10011, (212)633-3300, fax (212)463-5677, www. BarnesandNobleInc.com

   ▪ Barnes & Noble responds in 6-8 weeks. They will also tell you *why* they didn't accept your book if they decline it—in which case, you should craft a letter explaining why their reasoning is incorrect, and try again.

o New Vendor Acquisitions, Borders, 100 Phoenix
   Drive, Ann Arbor, MI   48108, (734)477-1111, fax
   (734)477-1313

   The Borders Group includes Waldenbooks and
   Brentanos, as well as Borders bookstores.   Borders
   will send you a postcard telling you whether your
   book has been accepted, and from which wholesaler
   they will be buying it.   They insist that all
   communication take place via mail, and don't disclose
   their buyer names, phone numbers, or email
   addresses.

o Books-A-Million, 402 Industrial Lane, Birmingham,
   AL 35211, (205)942-3737, fax (205)945-8586

   Books-A-Million chain also includes Wal-Mart chain
   now. They currently feature over 200 stores in 18
   states, with their heaviest concentration in the
   southeast.   They get most of their books from
   wholesaler American Wholesale Book Company,
   which doesn't seem to respond to mail
   communication, but you can fax the book buyer at
   (256)764-2511.

o In Canada, contact Chapters, 90 Ronson Drive,
   Etobicoke, ON   M9W-1C1, (416)243-3138, fax
   (416)243-8964.

Day Number 20

Today, you'll apply for Library of Congress **Cataloging in Publication (CIP)** data.

Request Cataloging in Publication Data

If you want your book to sell to libraries, you'll need cataloging in publication data. Here's how to get it:

- The Library of Congress in Washington oversees two programs (PCN and CIP) to facilitate the way libraries nationwide acquire and catalog books. Both programs assign a unique identification number to the catalog record for each book in its catalogued collections. The two programs are mutually exclusive: Once a book has a PCN it is ineligible for CIP data.

- PCN stands for Preassigned Card Number. (This is the Library of Congress's new term for an LCCN (Library of Congress Cataloging Number) that is preassigned. You can still get an LCCN, even years after the book is printed, if you never received any other cataloging for it.) CIP stands for Cataloging in Publication. Both facilitate cataloging. The main difference between the two is that the catalog record of books with CIP data is distributed to libraries, book dealers, and bibliographic networks worldwide (via the Library of Congress' Machine Readable Cataloging [MARC] Distribution Service) to facilitate orders and cataloging. Cataloging information for books with just a PCN is *available*—but is not distributed. A second difference is that the CIP data includes the desired Dewey and LC classification numbers; the PCN does not.

- All books acquired by libraries will need either the PCN or the CIP data. Libraries prefer CIP data—and are more likely to purchase books that contain CIP data than PCNs—because the cataloging records are already prepared. Furthermore, certain libraries buy books in certain CIP categories *sight unseen* each year. Even Baker & Taylor gets their notification of new titles via the Library of Congress' CIP records. Obviously, it is in your best interests to acquire the CIP data, rather than the PCN.

- The Library of Congress, however, is reluctant to open the CIP program to self publishers (and offers the PCN as a second-rate substitute). The eligibility for the CIP program states: "Only U.S. publishers who publish titles that are likely to be widely acquired by U.S. libraries are eligible to participate in the CIP program. Self-publishers (i.e. authors and editors who pay for or subsidize publication of their own works) and publishers who mainly publish the works of only one or two authors are ineligible. Publishers ineligible for the CIP program may be eligible for the PCN Program."

- There is (of course) a way around the Library of Congress's obstructions, and that is to present yourself as a big publishing house: Along with your request for CIP data, submit your forthcoming titles list.

- Bear in mind that even fiction can benefit from the inclusion of CIP data, particularly now that the Library of Congress has expanded their practice of putting genre headings in cataloging data.

- Send your application to: Library of Congress, Attention: New CIP Participant, Cataloging in Publication Division, 101 Independence Avenue S.E., Washington, DC 20540-4320. You can also submit your material online at `cip.loc.gov/cip/ecipp14.html` and `cip.loc.gov/cip/ecip8.html`.

- If you choose to pursue the less attractive PCN data, you can submit your application to `pcn.loc.gov/pcn`.

- Canadians can get CIP data in ten days by filling in the online form or by writing to the CIP Coordinator, National Library of Canada, 395 Wellington Street, Ottawa, ON K1A-ON4, (819)994-6881, fax (819)997-7517, `cip@NLC-BNC.ca`, `www.NLC-BNC.ca`

- Send the following information:

  o Name, address, and homepage of the publisher

  o Names, titles, email addresses, and phone numbers of the principal officers (Be sure you provide information on several officers.)

  o ISBN numbers, book titles, and (several different) authors

  o Evidence that the publisher is not self-publishing works authored by the publisher, and evidence that the publisher intends to publish the works of more than one or two authors, including photocopies of *just the front matter* of several forthcoming books.

o   Evidence that the books will be marketed to a broad segment of the library market

o   Catalogs or other promotional material

- The initial application to the Library of Congress will take at least 30 days. Cataloging of subsequent books should take only two weeks, although the recent anthrax scare has the Library of Congress backed up for several months. Try to submit everything online to avoid delays.

- If you are having difficulties and need to speak to someone in person, you can email the following publisher liaisons at the CIP office:

Publisher	Liaison	Email
A-B	Schamell Padgett	spad@loc.gov
C-Do	Servon Gatewood	sgat@loc.gov
Dp-G	Cassandra Latney	clat@loc.gov
H-I	Nancy Andrews	nandrews@loc.gov

J-L	Dionne Simmons	dsim@loc.gov
M-N	Sherry McCoy	sgmcc@loc.gov
O-Pri	Tina Chubbs	tchu@loc.gov
Prj-Saint	Patricia Dyson	pdys@loc.gov
S	Lynn Souder	csou@loc.gov
T-U	Regina Thomas	mthomas@loc.gov
V-Z	Sonya Stewart	sste@loc.gov

- Keep in mind that it may take several days (or weeks) to get a response to your email. For problems specifically relating to electronically-submitted CIP and PCN, contact David Bucknum at dabu@loc.gov.

- Quality Books, a non-exclusive distributor to libraries, also offers unofficial cataloging information for a fee, designed for publishing houses that haven't allowed enough time to get their cataloging data (or who can't get into the CIP program). Using Quality's cataloging, however, signals that your publishing house is small. Contact them at Quality Books, 1003 West Pines Road,

Oregon, IL 61061, (815)732-4450 or (800)323-4241, fax (815)732-4499, Carolyn.Olson@Quality-Books.com.

- Or, get your cataloging information block from any friendly librarian who knows how to do it. (Don't call it CIP data if you go this route, since it's not generated by the Library of Congress.)

- Once you receive your cataloging information, print it exactly as written on the copyright page of your book.

- The Library of Congress also issues copyrights. Your book is automatically copyrighted once you complete it—but you're still supposed to register it with the Library of Congress. The copyright protects everything in the text, including words and art, for your lifetime plus 50 years. The only thing not copyrighted is the title (which anyone can use.) As soon as you have printed books, you'll register the copyright. Today, write and request form TX from: Register of Copyrights, Library of Congress, Washington, DC   20559, (202)707-9100, lcweb.loc.gov/copyright.

This week you:

- **Chose an editor**

- **Finalized your manuscript**

- **Sent advance galleys to reviewers**

- **Sent advance galleys to chain stores**

- **Requested cataloging-in-publication data**

Congratulations! You're getting there!

Week Number Five

CR ℞

This week you'll:

- Lay out your book

- Plan your front matter

- Plan your back matter

- Locate a printer

- Submit RFQs to printers

Day Number 21

Today, you'll begin planning the **layout of your book**.

Lay Out Your Book

- Professional typographers and layout artists can propel your book from amateur to professional. If you're considering having your book's interior designed, consider the following interior layout artists:

    o Mayapriya Long, BookWrights, 2255 Westover Drive #108, Charlottesville, VA   22901, (804)823-8223, www.BookWrights.com

    o Pete Masterson, Aeonix Publishing Group, PO Box 20985, El Sobrante, CA   94820, (510)222-6743, Pete@Aeonix.com, www.Aeonix.com

    o Barry Kerrigan, DeskTop Miracles, 112 South Main Street, Stowe, VT   05672, (802)253-7900, fax (802)253-1900,   Barry@DeskTopMiracles.com, www.DeskTopMiracles.com

    o Pamela Terry of Opus 1 Design, PO Box 3653, Beverly Hills, CA   90212, (800)590-7778, fax (323)934-2881

- If you're going to lay your book out yourself, read a good book on the basics of design—Robin Williams' *The Non-Designer's Design Book* and Roger C. Parker's *One-Minute Designer* are my favorites. After you've immersed in the basics of good design, consider the following two approaches:

o One is to do your own layout in your favorite word processing package. The advantage is you already know your word processing package; the disadvantage is that standard word processing software results in poorly spaced type for books, and this causes reader fatigue. If you need help choosing an appropriate font for the book, check out the "Esperfonto" section of www.will-harris.com. If you insist on doing the typography with your word processor, be aware of these most common potential errors:

- Funky fonts. Professionals use one of the standard fonts, with serifs (the extensions on the top and bottoms of the letters) that lead the eye from one letter to the next, making the text easier to read. Only amateurs use sans-serif (without serif) fonts in the text of their books. Equally difficult to read are typefaces that have very thin, horizontal serifs, such as Bodoni and Ultra. Garamond and Bookman are both good serif fonts, as are Goudy, Palatino, Minion, Weiss, Utopia, Berkeley, and Baskerville. For children's books, typefaces such as New Century Schoolbook and Clarendon have a clean look.

- Boring fonts. Equally as bad as bizarre fonts are the ubiquitous fonts. Try to avoid the most overused fonts (particularly Times and Times New Roman) as well as Arial/Helvetica, which is used for IRS documents; all of these fonts are so common that they now seem almost unprofessional. Comic Sans and Tahoma are also poor choices.

- Poorly-combined fonts. If you're using more than one font, be sure they combine well. For example, fonts like Optima don't combine well with other fonts—because they incorporate too many similarities of both serif and sans serif fonts. And please—don't use too many fonts. (More than two is usually too many.)

- Be sure the type is large enough. Type that is too small is hard to read—and America is increasingly nearsighted. If the "x-height" of the font is too small—that is, the ratio of the small letter height to the capital letter height—then the font needs to be set bigger to be readable. Garamond, for example, will be difficult for many people to read in smaller than 12 point, because it has a small x-height; Minion, on the other hand, is much more readable in smaller point sizes, such as 11 points, as is Palatino.

- Be sure the type is not too large. Some fonts are just larger than others, so what works in one font may be too big in another. A general rule of thumb is to use 11 point type, but be sure it works in the font you've selected.

- Try Adobe (www.Adobe.com) or Bitstream (www.Bitstream.com) for their high-quality fonts. Try www.FontSite.com for a collection of inexpensive typefaces. Avoid bargain-basement fonts, as your printer may have trouble getting them to work well with their imagesetter (the typesetting device they use to produce very high-resolution output on paper or film).

- Be sure your design elements contrast. Don't use two fonts that appear incredibly similar—they'll be jarring, rather than pleasing, to the eye. (So, for example, don't use two fonts—even two serif fonts—on the same page, unless they're from different type families.) Similarly, don't use font sizes that are too similar: 12 point type will look better with 8 point than 11 point type.

- Traditional wisdom dictates putting only *one* space after all periods, not two. (Do a global search and replace throughout your document if you are accustomed to typing in two spaces.)

- Be sure to use what are called "typographer's quotes" rather than "straight quotes" for both quotations as well as apostrophes. (These are typographer quotes: " ". These are straight quotes: " ".)

- Don't use all caps.

- Be sure to leave enough white space or margin around your text. Leave a small margin between the text on facing pages; a little more between the top of the page and where the text starts on the top of the page; still a little more between the left and right borders of the pages and the text; and the most white space between the bottom of the text and the bottom of the pages.

- To prepare your word-processed text for the printer, you'll need to convert it into a file format they can use. Adobe PDF is the most common portable format; it works with virtually everything.

  ◆ A PDF reader (Acrobat® Reader) is free on the Adobe website, but if you want to create your own PDF files from your documents, you'll need to buy their Acrobat product. Or, you can use Adobe's file conversion service for $9.95 per month (cancelable at any time); you can try it for free five times. Check it out at `createpdf.adobe.com`. Ask your printer for the proper settings to use when converting your document to PDF.

  ◆ There are also freeware programs that can create PDF documents. Ghostscript and GSview are companion programs that allow you to convert a Postscript file into PDF, and view both Postscript and PDF documents. To use these, you first create a Postscript file from your document by "printing" it to a Postscript printer and saving the output to a file (using the Print to File option). Ghostscript then reads the Postscript, and can convert it into PDF (or other file formats). GSview is the companion viewer that can display Postscript and PDF documents; it also provides a graphical user interface to Ghostscript. You can get both from `www.cs.wisc.edu/~ghost/`. The best Postscript printer to use for this purpose is

the Adobe Postscript Printer Driver, which
you can get from www.adobe.com/support/
downloads/main.html (Select Printer
Drivers, and choose the right one for your
system.)

- Beware that many printers don't support
TrueType (Microsoft brand) fonts. Postscript
Type 1 fonts are the fonts most commonly
supported by printers. If you use TrueType fonts,
check with your printer to see if they can deal
with them.

- Before submitting your file to Adobe for PDF
conversion, make sure that the fonts you use are
supported by their converter (see their website for
a specific list.) If you're having problems creating
a PDF file that exactly matches your document,
try saving your file with the fonts embedded
(usually an option you select, e.g. for Microsoft
Word 2002: Tools→Options→Save→Embed
TrueType Fonts). See www.adobe.com/
support/techdocs/28006.htm for tips on
producing PDF files from Microsoft Word
documents.

- Be sure that you only use fonts that are actually
installed on your system. On a PC, for example,
you can look at your fonts folder
(Start→Settings→Control Panel→Fonts) to see
which fonts you have installed (though some
applications install fonts in other places). For
example, if you use Garamond font in your

document, and then make some text both bold and italic, you should make sure you have Garamond Bold Italic font installed. If you only have Garamond Bold and Garamond Italic fonts, but not Garamond Bold Italic, your word processor will make its own version of Garamond Bold Italic, which may not be consistent when printed on a different printer. This can cause "reflow" problems, that is, some text may be larger or smaller (because the missing made-up font displays or prints slightly larger or smaller), which can cause that text to move ("reflow") to a different line or page, changing the layout of the document. This can make your table of contents or index wrong, add a page so that you no longer have the right number of pages, or cause other problems. See `www.adobe.com/support/techdocs/f366.htm` for other tips on dealing with reflow problems.

- Alternatively, you can submit camera-ready copy to your printer, particularly if your text has no graphics. Just set your printer's dpi (dots per inch resolution) to as high a number as possible, but you'll need at least 600dpi for text, possibly more for pages that contain graphics (photographs or line drawings). Check with your printer for the proper resolution settings for their press.

o The preferred option is to use a page layout program, specifically designed for book layout. You'll end up with a more professional product, although you will have the initial expense and learning curve. Of the software programs on the market, Adobe PageMaker® and InDesign®, and Quark, Inc.'s QuarkXpress® are generally considered to be the best overall for book layout. InDesign is newer, compatible with PageMaker, and can read QuarkXPress files. The Adobe "Publishing" or "Design" collections include the software tools you'll need for about $1,000.

The best way to end up with a layout that you like for your book is to go to a bookstore and seek out a book that looks right to you. In the long run, this will save you more time than messing around with all the options and trying to figure it out on your own. In preparing your book for the printer, keep in mind the following points:

- Start text a third or halfway down the page after a new chapter title.

- Use clip art to set chapter titles off from the text.

- Consider using large capital letters at the beginning of chapters; it looks particularly snazzy.

- Consider starting each chapter on a right-hand page.

- Sprinkle subheads liberally throughout your (non-fiction) book. People find it difficult to read large blocks of uninterrupted text, and subheads make it easier for them to find sections they're looking for.

- Build in sufficient margins, so your text doesn't look crowded. Make sure you put in a little extra room for the bottom border.

- Don't forget to include page numbers!

- Art or photographs should always go *after* you talk about them.

Day Number 22

Today, you'll put together the **front matter** for your book.

Plan Your Front Matter

The front matter of your book is the series of pages before the book actually starts—the title page, the copyright page, the table of contents, dedication, etc. Here are the elements of your book's front matter:

- The inside front cover (also called the *flyleaf* or *end paper* in hardcover books.) This page can be left blank or printed upon. (In this book, it's blank.)

- Half-Title Page. This first page usually includes the title and publishing house name. In mass market books, this page also includes promotional materials or endorsements. (In this book, it's the "Here's what experts are saying..." page.)

- Backside (verso) of Half-Title Page. This second page of the book traditionally lists the author's previous books. Sometimes it lists other titles (related to the subject matter) published by the same press. (In this book, it's actually the continuation of endorsements from the previous page, and I've moved the book information to a later page. None of this is carved in stone.)

- Title page. On this page, most books list the title, author, publisher, and publishing house logo. (You can find this on what would, if numbered, be page 7 in this book; because my endorsements take up four full pages, I inserted an extra page for my other books, the back of which was left blank.)

- Copyright page. This is traditionally the reverse side of the title page, (in this book it's page 8) and includes the following:

  o At the very top, write: Copyright © 2003 by Your Name. Printed in the United States of America

  o The words "All rights reserved. No part of this book may be reproduced or transmitted in any form or by any means, electronic or mechanical, including photocopying, recording, or by any information storage and retrieval system without written permission from the publisher, except for the inclusion of brief quotations in a review."

  o Next, include any information you'd like to give the reader about quantity purchases or special offers. Here are some possibilities of what you might offer in this section:

    ▪ An email newsletter that you publish on related topics

    ▪ More information or resources on your topic (available at your website or elsewhere)

    ▪ An offer to corporations or other organizations who might like to purchase the book in quantity for use as fundraisers or premiums o Next, list the complete contact information for the publishing house. Include:

- Publishing house name

- Street address, city, state, zip

- Telephone/fax

- Email address

- Web address

- SAN number if you have one. (You only need a SAN if you have multiple locations.)

o On the next few lines, include the Library of Congress cataloging information. It should look like this:

Library of Congress Cataloging-in-Publication Data

Your Last Name, Your First Name

Title of book—only first word is capitalized

/ by your first name and last name.

p. cm.

Includes bibliographical references and index.

ISBN 1-000000-00-0

1. Include the CIP information here.

- o Finally, specify the printing; Either include the words "First Printing") or simply include the string of numbers (in order, or in reverse order) from one to ten. (When you get to the second printing, you simply remove the number '1' from the string. This is an artifact from the days before computers, when this information was stripped in by hand to eliminate excessive copy changes, which were expensive. The graphic person at the printer simply sliced out the numbers with a razor blade, and reshot that section of the text.)

- Dedication. Make sure to make this as interesting as possible—people really do read these! And don't forget, this is a great place to thank people who were particularly helpful to you.

- Foreword. (Don't misspell this word: It's *Foreword*, not *Forward*!) This introduction to your book by an expert in the field offers the book credibility—and will enhance its sales.

- Preface. Here's your chance to introduce the book yourself. This is where most readers start—so make this section count! It should be representative in style and tone of the rest of the book, and should be punchy, interesting, and if at all possible and appropriate, humorous.

- Table of Contents. Most bookstore browsers will leaf through the table of contents to see if there's anything that interests them—so make your chapter titles interesting and provocative! Keep them relatively short.

- List of illustrations. This is also an artifact of a prior era. Except for academic publications with lots of figures and tables, there's really no reason to include a list of the illustrations—except that people have grown to expect it.

Day Number 23

Today, you'll put together the **back matter** for your book.

Plan Your Back Matter

If you want your book to sell well to libraries, consider adding back matter. Libraries, in particular, appreciate books that have one or more appendices, a bibliography, a glossary, and an index, in that order. Most non-fiction books benefit from having one or more of these elements, so why not plan to include them in yours? Here's what can go in the back of the book:

- An appendix is useful for codifying any information that doesn't fit neatly into the format of the rest of the book. For example, since this book follows the 30-day model, anything that didn't fit into that system—sample budgets, for example—was included in the appendix. Long lists, such as contact lists, or reference material, also work well in the appendix. Have one appendix for each type of information you're including in the back; some books have many appendices.

- Some books include a few blank pages labeled *Notes*. In some books, it's appropriate to include such blank pages; in some books it's not. Often these pages are just included as a way of bringing the page count up to a multiple of 8 or 16 pages, referred to as a "signature" in the book printing business; it's usually cheaper to print books when the page count is a multiple of 8 or 16 pages, because of the vagaries of printing presses.

- A glossary is useful for any book that has terms that might be unfamiliar to the average reader. If your book covers an industry or pastime with a lot of jargon or lingo, consider a glossary so that your readers can look up words they don't know without continually resorting to a dictionary. (Another approach is to skip the glossary, and simply define the words as they appear in the book.)

- A bibliography or recommended reading list can be useful in directing readers to other, related books. If you've written several books on a similar topic, use a bibliography to direct readers to your other publications!

- A good index can make it easier for readers to locate the information in your book. (A poorly designed index, on the other hand, is of benefit to no one.) You can do the index yourself—most word processing and page layout software have this capability—or you can let a professional tackle it. The problem (art) of indexing is not in the typography of the index, which any word processor can do; it's in knowing how to write the index entries, and how to categorize them. This is the expertise that a professional brings to the project.

  o To find a professional indexer in your area, see the list in *Literary Marketplace*.

  o You can locate an indexer online at www.indexer locator.org.

- o   Or contact the American Society of Indexers, (303)463-2887, fax (303)422-8894, `info@AS Indexing.org`, `www.ASIndexing.org`

- o   Or contact the American Society of Indexers (info above) for their free "Indexing Guide for Editors" and do the indexing yourself.

- o   To find out more about indexing in general, subscribe to the mailing list, Index-L. Send email to: `Lyris@Listserv.UNC.edu`. In the body of the message (not the subject header) write: *Subscribe Index-L your-first-name your-last-name*.

- Most books include a biography of the author. If you've included the author's biography on the back cover, you might consider a longer biography here; or you can eliminate this additional biography entirely. You should also consider an author photograph on this page, if it does not appear on the back cover. If you want readers to write to you directly, you may also want to include the author contact information (address or email) on this page.

- The last (even) page of all books should be an order form. Why miss this one last chance to suggest that readers buy your books? If you're planning to do a follow-on book, include the ordering information for that book as well to maximize your marketing power. Don't forget to include information on how to order by telephone, mail, fax, and web (including your contact information) as well as the price, tax, and shipping fees. Some self publishers say you shouldn't include an order form, for fear of alienating bookstores, who won't want customers ordering directly from you.   If you're concerned, suggest that the reader can buy the book at their local bookstore OR from you.

Day Number 24

Today, you'll locate a **printer**.

Locate Printers

Many first-time publishers make the same few mistakes when they're contracting for printing. In locating a printer, remember the following:

- Be sure you've edited your book *before* you send it to the printer. Inevitably, there are editorial changes that you don't notice until you're looking at the printer's proof. That, however, is not the time to make anything other than *essential* changes as each of those changes will cost you extra. So don't rush this stage; make sure you've allowed sufficient time to check, and re-check, your book before it goes to the printer.

- Don't use a local Quick Print Shop. Although everyone's inclination is to use their local Ma and Pa print shop, only a full-time book printer can give you the most competitive pricing. Out of thousands of printers in the U.S., fewer than a hundred specialize in printing books. Use a printer which does nothing but books: Their prices will be more competitive, and there will be fewer problems.

- Get multiple bids. Printing prices vary tremendously—and the only way to be sure you're getting the best price is by bidding your job to a number of different printers.

- One additional note on printing. There are two schools of thought on subsequent printings. One says that you should always bid your jobs out—to determine the cheapest price, each time you go back to print. The other school of thought is, once you find a printer whose prices are reasonable and whose work you like, stick with him. The few dollars you may save by shopping it around will be more than offset by the enhanced customer service you'll receive from a printer whose work you use again and again and again. Also, it can take time to "debug" the printing process for your books—getting the file formats to produce the results you want, finding exactly the right paper, and so forth. Once you've gone through this once, with one printer, you might want to think twice about doing the whole thing again with a different printer!

- Learn more about printing. The more educated you are about the printing process, the better questions you'll ask, and the better print job you'll receive. Here are two suggestions:

  o The best book I've ever seen on the entire printing process is Helmut Kipphan's *Handbook of Print Media.* It was just translated into English, contains over a thousand pages, weighs a lot, and is prohibitively expensive, but definitely worth examining (at your local library); it is much too detailed in some areas, and completely not detailed in others, to make purchasing it justifiable.

  o *The Pocket Pal* has been in print for eons, and is incredibly detailed (250 pages), including a glossary of industry terms. You can get it from International

Paper Company at `www.ippocketpal.com` for $12.95.

- Below is a list of the top book printers in the U.S. Be sure to submit your RFQ (discussed tomorrow) to several of them, to get the best pricing and terms.

  o Bang Printing, 1473 Highway 18, Brainerd, MN 56401, (800)328-0450, fax (218)829-7145, `BangInfo@BangPrinting.com`, `www.BangPrinting.com`

  o Bertelsmann, 28210 North Avenue, Stanford, Valencia, CA 91355, (888)564-0001, `Penny.Hancock@BisUs.com`, `www.bisus.com`

  o BookMasters, 2541 Ashland Road, Mansfield, OH 44905, (800)537-6727, fax (419)589-4040, `info@BookMasters.com`, `www.BookMasters.com`

  o Central Plains Book Manufacturing, PO Box 738, Arkansas City, KS 67005, (877)278-2726, fax (316)221-4762, `BookPrinter@MyFirstLink.net`, `www.CentralPlainsBook.com`

  o CJ Krehbiel, 3962 Virginia Avenue, Cincinnati, OH 45227, (800)598-7808, fax (513)271-6082, `www.CJKrehbiel.com`

  o Color House Graphics, 3505 Eastern Avenue, Grand Rapids, MI 49508, (616)241-1916, fax (616)245-5494, `CHG@Iserv.net` o Courier Corporation, 5 Wellman Avenue, N. Chelmsford, MA 01863, (978)251-6000, fax (978)251-8228, www.Courier.com

o Data Reproductions, 4545 Glenmeade Lane, Auburn Hills, MI 48326, (800)242-3114, fax (248)371-3702, www.DataRepro.com

o DeHart's Printing, 3265 Scott Boulevard, Santa Clara, CA 95054, (888)982-4763, fax (408)982-9912, www.DeHarts.com

o Fidlar Doubleday, 6255 Technology Avenue, Kalamazoo, MI 49009, (800)632-2259, fax (888)999-0655, www.Fidlar.com

o Hignell Book Printing, 488 Burnell Street, Winnipeg, MB R3G-2B4, Canada, (800)304-5553, fax (204)774-4053, www.Hignell.mb.ca

o King Printing, 171 Swan Street, Lowell, MA 01852, www.KingPrinting.com

o Malloy, 5411 Jackson Road, Ann Arbor, MI 48103, (800)722-3231, fax (707)745-2175, www.Malloy.com

o Maple-Vail, PO Box 2695, York, PA 17405, (717)764-5911, fax (717)764-4702, www.Maple-Vail.com

o McNaughton & Gunn, 960 Woodland Drive, Saline, MI 48176, (800)677-2665, fax (800)677-2665, www.McNaughton-Gunn.com

o Pacific Rim International Printing, 11726 San Vicente Boulevard #280, Los Angeles, CA 90049, (800)952-6567, fax (310)207-2566, www.PacRim-Intl.com

o Phoenix Color, 540 Western Maryland Parkway, Hagerstown, MD   21740, (301)733-0018, www. PhoenixColor.com

o Quebecor World, 1989 Arcata Boulevard, Martinsburg, WV   25402, (304)267-3600, fax (304)267-0989, www.QuebecorWorld.com

o Rose Printing, 2503 Jackson Bluff Road, Tallahassee, FL   32304, (800)227-3725, fax (850)576-4153, www. RosePrinting.com

o R. R. Donnelley, 77 W. Wacker Drive, Chicago, IL 60601, (312)326-8000, www.RRDonnelley.com

o Sheridan Books, 613 E. Industrial Drive, Chelsea, MI 48118, (800)999-2665, fax (734)475-7337, www. SheridanBooks.com

- Once you've zeroed-in on a printer, try sending your RFQ to a print broker to see if he can underbid. In general, brokers are not recommended; if there are problems with the print job, it may be difficult to resolve them when you're working with both a printer and a broker. On the other hand, a responsible print broker can get you much better pricing, and excellent customer service. My favorite is Ron Pramschufer, Books Just Books, 51 East 42nd Street, New York, NY   10017, (800)621-2556, RJComm@aol.com, www.BooksJust Books.com. A good print broker can often bid lower on jobs than even the most competitive printer.

Day Number 25

Today you'll submit a **Request for Quotation** to printers.

Submit RFQs to Printers

Today you'll submit RFQs to printers. RFQ is industry lingo for "Request for Quotation," and is a way of inviting printers to bid on your book printing, as a way of determining who can give you the best price. Keep in mind that RFQ responses are generally good for a short period of time (two to six weeks, usually); beyond that, paper prices and other costs may fluctuate, causing the bid to go up or down.

- On your publishing house letterhead, write the words "Request for Quotation" followed by your book title.

- Now, determine the specifics of your particular print job. Here are some things to consider:

  o Do you want hardcover or softcover? Traditionally, reviewers and libraries were less interested in softcover books (reviewers would only review hardcovers, libraries would only purchase hardcovers.) Today, however, many publishers opt for publishing in softcover exclusively. Hardcover generally costs only $1-$3 more per book to print, though you do run into additional costs in cover design as well (because the dust jacket has flaps, so it's bigger—more cover to design.)

o   If you're printing softcover, what sort of binding do you want? Most publishers opt for perfect binding, where the cover is glued on. Perfect binding is generally the least expensive, and the most versatile. Other bindings—including comb, wire, side stitched, and saddle stitched—have a lower perceived value and are disliked by libraries and bookstores, because you can't read the title on the spine. Otta-Bind™ and Lay-Flat™ bindings (which are used for things like cookbooks, because you can open them and they'll stay open without being held) are more expensive. Hardcover binding is even more expensive (add at least $1-$3 additional per book) but since it is perceived to have a much higher value, you can mark it up significantly in price. In general, however, unless you have an exceptional book or exceptional reason, stick with perfect binding.

o   What sort of finish do you want? Most softcovers have a gloss finish, but for certain books (such as those small, cozy books near the checkout counters) matte can be more appropriate, though it's usually more expensive than glossy laminate. (Avoid UV coating: It's not a laminate, but a water-based coating that won't protect the book the way laminate will.) Specify lay-flat laminate to avoid humidity curling. Matte PLC (printed, laminated covers) can be a cleaner look for a hardcover than a dust jacket, at a slightly lower price, but gloss PLC tends to scratch easily.

o   Do you want to use a combination, like spot-gloss over matte finish? The spot-gloss highlights only certain key parts of the cover for special effect. Talk to your cover designer if you think this is appropriate.

o   Do you want to emboss the front cover to emphasize certain words or give pictures a 3-dimensional appearance? Again, talk to your cover designer if you're interested in this, and be aware that the printing costs will be higher.

o   What ink do you want? (Black is cheapest; color gets pricey.)

o   What color paper stock do you want?   (Most publishers print on white; I print some of my books on natural stock, which I find easier on the eyes. Keep in mind that dye lots may vary from printer to printer and job to job.)

o   What thickness of paper do you want? In general, heavier paper is more expensive. (Look at the weight of the paper—most printers use 50#, 55#, and 60# white and natural offset paper for books—and also the PPI, or pages per inch, of the paper you're considering; the greater the PPI, the thinner the pages. (If you're used to discussing paper weights at copy shops, 20# bond is the same as 50# offset, and 24# bond is the same as 60# offset.) If you're trying to make a smallish book appear bigger, go for a lower PPI, and vice versa. Most printers will have several "stock" paper choices that are substantially cheaper than the rest; to save money, use the printer's stock paper. (Be sure to notify your cover artist of the width as soon as you've selected a paper thickness. To calculate the spine width of your book, divide the

total number of pages by the PPI, and then add the
thickness of the two covers. Since this will vary by
cover stock selected, be sure to check with the printer
to get an accurate spine width.)

> [Do *not* buy your own paper, as some self-
> publishing experts suggest. Manufacturers buy
> paper in bulk, resulting in the lowest possible
> price. Don't waste your time trying to find a
> lower price. Also, printers hate small publishers
> that come with their own paper—that loss of
> profit margin will just turn up elsewhere in your
> bill, guaranteed.]

o What sort of finish do you want? Coffee table books
   are usually printed on glossy paper; matte finish is
   also available.

o What thickness of cover do you want? Most books
   today are done in what is called 10-point C1S cover
   stock (one point of cover stock is the same as 1/72
   of an inch, and C1S means coated on one side—that
   is, the outside is glossy, while the inside cover is
   uncoated.) You can also opt for 12-point cover stock
   for a slightly richer, heavier feel. Hardcover books
   often use an 80-100 lb. dust jacket.

o How many books do you want to print? The more
   books you print, the cheaper the cost. Printing 1000
   200-page books can cost $2.50 per book; printing
   3000 can bring that price down to $2, and printing
   5,000 books can bring it down to $1.30. 3,000 books
   is considered an average small press print run. On
   the other hand, you don't want to print more than

your storage facility (garage, anyone?) can hold, and you certainly don't want to print more than you think you'll sell in the next six months. Keep in mind that whatever number you decide to print, printers, by convention, can charge you for an "overrun"; be sure to ask how much overrun is customary (generally 10%). (In other words, if you order 3,000 books you may receive, and end up having to pay for, 3,300 books.)

o How many pages is your book? Sheet-fed presses require multiples of 32 pages (32, 64, 96, 128, 160, 192, 224, 256, 288); the faster web presses require multiples of 48 pages (48, 96, 144, 192, 240, 288). If you can keep your page numbers to one of the above multiples (what is called an even number of signatures) you will generally get much cheaper pricing than if you submit an "uneven" number. Consider adding blank pages or extra order forms in the back to get this magic multiple. If your book is 96, 192, or 288 pages you won't have to worry about whether you'll be printing on a web or sheet fed press.

o What size book (what "trim size") do you want? Think carefully about the type of book you are producing to determine the size. A typical popular size (because it's cheapest to produce for most printers) is 5.5" x 8.5". But if you're printing a cookbook, for example, or a coffee table book, you may want a larger size; standard cookbook size is 7" by 10". If you're printing a "cozy" inspirational book, you may opt for a smaller size, such as 5.5" by 6.5".

[Consider standardizing your trim size for all the subsequent books you produce. It's most cost-effective, and you'll find it easier to fulfill orders if all books are the same size, all cartons contain the same quantity, etc.]

o How many illustrations will your book have? Simple black and white line drawings are inexpensive to add to your book; adding photographs (which, because of their grey scale, require the production of a halftone) cost a bit more. (You can do this with your word-processing or page-layout software for free; it's only more money if you expect the printer to do it for you. If you submit the entire interior of the book as a PDF file, photos do not add to the cost.) Color pictures, for most books, are not very cost-effective; even a few pages of interior color will add at least $1-$5 to the per book cost, in quantities of 1,000 to 3,000 books.

o Do you want the books to be shrink wrapped? Shrink wrapping will help protect books stored under adverse conditions (there's that garage again) and will reduce damage in shipping. Many publishers opt for a combination of shrinking in bundles of five (to mail to wholesalers) and shrink wrapping singles (to send to direct mail customers.) Shrink wrapping generally costs about 15-25 cents each.

o Do you want to purchase "extra covers" for use in publicity? The printer can usually throw these in for a low cost.

o What kind of proofs do you require? (Color? Laser copy?) If exact color matching is critical, ask your printer to provide you with the best color-accurate proofs. You'll also likely need to use the sophisticated color-matching capabilities of high-end book design software, which is beyond the scope of this book.

o How will you submit your book? If you're submitting electronically, make sure your printer supports the exact same version of software you use, and has the same fonts you use (better yet, be sure to include all of the font files you use with the files you submit.)

- As camera-ready copy? (i.e. Actual paper pages)

- Electronic copy direct from your application? (e.g. QuarkXPress, InDesign, Pagemaker, Word)

- Electronic copy in a portable format? (e.g. PDF, Postscript)

Review Day Number 21 for more information on how to prepare your book for the printer.

o How do you want your books packed? Specify cartons with at least 275 lb. burst strength to ensure strong boxes. Ask them to ensure that there is enough packing so that you can ship the books out to wholesalers in the original packaging, saving you a great deal of repacking time. If you have particular ideas on pallets and packaging, specify those in your RFQ. We tell our printers to keep the number of books per carton constant (which also serves to keep the boxes at a constant, and optimal weight of between 30-40 lbs) and to stack the boxes on pallets in an interlocking pattern.   The pallets are then plastic-wrapped to keep the cartons together. Similarly, standardize your pallet counts, so wholesalers can order in pallet quantities easily.   We shrink-wrap the books in groups of five.   (For subsequent print runs, be sure to specify that the number of books per box should be the same as you got in your first print run, since that info is used by wholesalers and distributors to size their orders, and is troublesome to change once they've entered it into their databases.) Ask the printer to label the ends of the boxes with the name of the book, quantity of books per box, and ISBN number; this will make it easier for you to distinguish boxes of books in your garage or warehouse.

o   What terms do you need? For your first print run, many printers will require prepayment in full or in part. For subsequent print jobs with the same printer, you should be able to obtain net 30 day terms. Ask if the printer can reduce the final price if you prepay, pay promptly, or change anything else on your specifications.

o   What's the charge for shipping? Find out how much your printer charges for shipping.   (Put "FOB destination" on your RFQ to make sure they calculate that into their quote. That means "Free on Board," that is, the party specified does *not* pay the shipping charges.)   Some printers may be able to drop ship directly to your wholesaler. Find out how heavy your cartons will be, so you can get quotes on your shipping costs. Don't forget that several of the small press organizations, including PMA and SPAN, offer discount rates to members for shipping charges.

o   What sort of turn-around time do you need? (You can get lower prices, usually, if you're not in a rush.) Don't plan to have books by a particular date unless you have an arrival date guaranteed in writing.

* Next, type up your specifications. Be sure to add a line at the bottom of the RFQ that says "RFQ takes precedence over industry convention" to make sure you get exactly what you anticipate. Now fax or email copies of your RFQ to several printers on the preceding list, all of whom have worked happily with independent publishers. (More printers can be found on Pete Masterson's excellent website, www.Aeonix.com.) As a general rule, digital printers are best if you're printing under 1000 books, if your trim size is less than 8.5 by 11, if you're printing in black ink, if you're printing on standard paper weights (50, 60, or 70 #), or if you don't require high quality photo resolution; offset printing is best for quantities over 1000 books, if you're printing in color, if you require non-standard paper weights, or if you require high quality photo reproduction.

* In general, in evaluating printer bids remember to carefully check the bids against your submitted requirements, and make sure your selected printer commits to differences and changes *in writing* before you commit to the job.

208 Week Number Five

This week you:

- **Laid out your book**

- **Planned your front matter**

- **Planned your back matter**

- **Located a printer**

- **Submitted RFQs**

Congratulations! You're almost done!

Week Number Six

☙ ❧

This week you'll:

- Do a final pre-print check

- Submit your book to the printer

- Ship your books from the printer

- List your book and publishing house

- Organize your shipping department

- Review and renew your business plan

- Plan for the next book

Day Number 26

Today you'll do a **final check** of necessary components before you send your book to the printer, and **submit your book** to the printer.

Do a Pre-Print Final Check

Before you send your document to the printer, check the following items:

- Be sure your cover designer has done the spine to the correct width. The way to figure the spine width is to divide the number of pages in your book by the PPI (pages per inch) of the paper you've chosen, and then add in the thickness for the front and back cover. (Thus, for example, if your book is 200 pages, and your paper has a PPI of 400, the spine will be half an inch, plus the additional width of both covers.) Some printers also add a little bit to account for the air space between signatures and the effects of glue. As this will vary depending on the paper stock used, be sure to check with the printer.

- If you have changed *any* specification on your print quote, get a written confirmation of the change. (Sometimes what you think of as a small change will cause the price to increase significantly.)

- Plan to send your printer camera ready text and art, in addition to any disks. That will reduce the chances of a misunderstanding.

- Be sure your book contains all of the following elements:

  o Title page (title, author, publisher, website URL)

  o Copyright page (copyright author and date, ISBN, CIP data, printing number)

  o Front cover (title and author)

  o Spine (title, author, and publishing house)

  o Back cover (title, author, ISBN and barcode, price, subject/shelving information, quotes or endorsements)

- Make sure that you have inserted information on *all* your books and upcoming related products on the book's order form, which should be printed as the last page of the book. This way you won't miss out on potential sales of current and future books and products.

- Make sure your author bio includes information on any consulting and speaking you do on your topic. That's free publicity for you—don't miss your chance!

- When the printer sends you proofs, look them over extremely carefully. If you need to make changes, now is the last (affordable) time. Send the proofs back immediately, so you don't hold up your production schedule.

Submit Your Book to the Printer

- If you are sending electronic files, be sure that they are in a format readable by your printer.

  o CDs are now ubiquitous and the recommended media for submitting files.

  o Make your CDs readable on both PCs and Macs by using ISO9660 format (not Joliet, a PC-only CD format).

  o Be sure to include all the fonts you used, and any separate image files.

  o Be sure to indicate the version numbers of your page layout or word-processing software.

- Send all materials—disks, camera-ready copy, etc—to the printer.

  o Send them with delivery confirmation or signature-required, so you know that they arrived safely.

  o Be sure to keep spare copies for yourself.

Day Number 27

Today you'll arrange to **ship your books** from the printer back to you.

Ship Your Books from the Printer

Once you know when your books will be printed, you need to arrange to have them shipped from the printer back to you. Here's how:

- Find out from your printer how heavy your cartons will be, so you can get quotes on your shipping costs.

- Check out the APA Transport website at www.apatransport.com to figure shipping costs to anywhere in the country. (Books are considered class 60 or 65.)

- Comparison shop with at least a few shipping companies; prices can vary tremendously. Consider:

  o Clipper Express, Margaret Clifton, (530)432-5521, owwnedson@aol.com, www.clippergroup.com/ nationalltl.asp. PMA discount.

  o Con-Way Central Express, (800)642-3238, www.con-way.com

  o Freight Management Systems, (865)922-7491, fax (865)922-7492, www.fmsamerica.com

- o Yellow Transportation, (913)344-3000, `webyfs@yellowcorp.com`, `www.yellowcorp.com`

- Call the shipping coordinator of the shipping company you've selected.

  - o Be sure you know the dimensions (height, width, depth and projected weight) of the shrink-wrapped skids, and the number of skids.

  - o Be sure to let the shipping company know that you are shipping books. (Shipping charges are based on National Motor Freight classifications. Books can be class 50, 60, or 65, but are usually shipped class 60 or 65.)

  - o You will need to let them know the originating (shipping) and receiving (destination) zip codes.

  - o Be sure you know when the books are arriving. Some companies offer a notify service, by which they call you a few hours in advance of the delivery, a service which can be extremely helpful if you are not always home all day. This may cost extra.

  - o Be sure that the shipper knows if they're shipping to a residential address; sometimes there are additional fees involved. Also, check to make sure that an 18-wheeler can drive down your street, that the power lines are not too low, and that there are no low bridges blocking access to your street or storage area.

  - o If you will need a fork-lift truck to get the books unloaded (that is, if they're going into your home or garage, and you don't own a loading dock) make sure you have booked one; there may be an additional charge. (Often, it can be cheaper to avoid booking the forklift truck, and instead simply pay the driver in cash to unload them on his own. The fork lift might run as high as $100; the driver is generally happy with anything over $25. But not all drivers in the world want to do this.)

- If you're using a fulfillment house, notify them of the books' arrival.

- Before your books arrive, consider purchasing insurance for them. If they will be living in a shed or your garage until they are sold, your books may experience problems with heat curl or mildew. Insurance may save you thousands of dollars in inventory.

- When your books arrive from the printer, be sure to check the number of cartons (to make sure that you've gotten the correct number) and the quality of the books (to make sure there are no obviously bent or damaged books.) Also, page through one or two copies of the books in each of several boxes to make sure everything is in the correct order; occasionally printers make mistakes, and pages can be in the wrong order, or missing. Check to make sure that the correct quantities are shrink-wrapped in bundles of fives and ones, if applicable. Check to make sure they've packed the books in the boxes you've specified, with sufficient packing material as you've specified.

Day Number 28

Today, you'll **announce your book** to several publishing directories, **list your book with online bookstores**, and **organize your shipping department**.

List Your Book and Publishing House

Now you should submit your book for inclusion in several important directories, as well as the online bookstores. Here's how to begin:

- You should already have listed your book on the ABI form on Day Number Eight.

- Be sure your book's information is listed correctly so that bookstores and libraries can find it. At the very least, make sure that Bowker/Books in Print has the correct information, and Baker and Taylor; email Julia Munoz at MunozJ@Btol.com (You can even have B&T fix your database errors if you are not distributed by them; just email the correct information to datafix@btol.com.)

- Literary Market Place. This book lists all major publishers and suppliers. To be officially listed, you must publish at least three books a year. Again, send your "Forthcoming Titles" and "Terms" to: Literary Market Place, 630 Central Avenue, New Providence, NJ 07974, (800)824-2470 or (908)771-7755, fax (908)665-2895, www. literarymarketplace.com.

- If you're a Canadian publisher, list with Book Trade in Canada, Quill & Quire, 70 The Esplanade #210, Toronto, ON M5E-1R2, Canada, (416)360-0044, fax (416)955-0794, www.QuillAndQuire

- Send a copy of your book to have it listed in *Cumulative Book Index*, an international directory of new books. Send to: *Cumulative Book Index*, H.W. Wilson Co., 950 University Avenue, Bronx, NY 10452, (800)367-6770, fax (800)590-1617, www.hwwilson.com.

- Remember to follow up with a printed copy of the book to the CIP office; they request this for final cataloging. (This is important if you want to make sure your book sells well to libraries.) Send your printed book to: The Library of Congress, Cataloging in Publication Division, 101 Independence Avenue S.E., Washington, DC 20540-4320.

- Now that you have a printed book, remember to register it for copyright. Send it with form TX (which you ordered on Day Number 12) and $30 to: Register of Copyrights, Library of Congress, Washington, DC 20559, (202)707-9100, lcweb.loc.gov/copyright/. A copyright does a few things for your book:

  o Although the act of creating the book copyrights it automatically, registering the copyright officially establishes a public record of the copyright claim, important if there is ever a violation of the copyright.

  o The copyright is valid from the moment of creation until 70 years after the creator's death.

o   The copyright protects the text and art in the book—
    everything except the title; titles can not be
    copyrighted.

- Send your finished book to all the reviewers who only
  accept finished books:

    o   *Choice*, 100 Riverview Center, Middletown, CT 06457,
        (860)347-1387, fax (860)346-8586

        Send only books appropriate to colleges and
        research libraries.

    o   John Culleton, *Rowse Reviews*, 2401 Haight Avenue,
        Eldersburg, MD 21784

    o   Jim Cox, *Midwest Book Review*, 278 Orchard Drive,
        Oregon, WI   53575, (608)835-7937, MBR@ExecPC
        .com, www.MidwestBookReview.com

    o   *Fearless Book Reviews*, 1678 Shattuck Avenue #319,
        Berkeley, CA 94709, Queries@FearlessBooks.com

List Your Book With Online Bookstores

List your book with all the online bookstores:

- To list with Amazon.com, here's what to do:

    o   Go to the Books homepage

    o   Scroll down and select *Publishers Guide*

    o   Select *Complete Instructions*

o Fill out the editorial information online. Keep in mind that all consumers will see, for the most part, is your top two or three reviewer comments. So make them count: Put *everything* that's important up there. I recommend including your email address or website in this area—so that customers can contact you directly with questions (or orders!)

o If you need to correct anything later, email book-typos@Amazon.com

o Next, send your book cover (not the whole book, just the cover to be scanned) to: Amazon.com Advantage Books, PO Box 80727, Seattle, WA 98108. (You can also ftp the cover to Amazon using the instructions on their Amazon Advantage web pages.)

o Send a review copy of the book to Amazon Editors, PO Box 81226, Seattle, WA 98108. Include a letter explaining why they should review your title.

o If your Amazon listing appears incorrectly, here's how to correct it: Sign in with your username and password, and go to *Correct Errors and Omissions in this Listing.* Corrections will appear online within 7 days.

• To list with BarnesAndNoble.com, here's what to do:

o Go to the bottom of the www.BarnesAndNoble.com screen and select *Publishers and Authors Guide*

o Click on *Establishing a Warehouse Relationship*

o Fill out the publisher information form

o Then go back and read *How to Submit Content* and *How to Sell Us Your New Books*

o BN.com will contact you within a few weeks

o Send any corrections to `Corrections@BarnesAnd Noble.com`

- To list with Books-A-Million, here's what to do:

    o Go to www.`BAMM.com`

    o At the bottom of the screen select *For Publishers* and follow the directions. (Do not select *Pub Center* which is Books-A-Million's i-Universe pay-to-publish-online equivalent.)

Organize Your Shipping Department

Your outgoing shipping is more important than it first appears. If you can't get books to your customers in an efficient, timely manner, and if the books don't arrive in good shape, you will not have happy customers. Here are some considerations in organizing your shipping operation:

- Before you ship books to *anyone*, make sure you have already been reviewed by any publications that are likely to review you. If you are hoping for a review from *Library Journal* or *Publishers Weekly*, don't ship books to Amazon until the review appears. The most prestigious review journals today check online listings before they print reviews; if your book is already listed at Amazon and BarnesAndNoble.com, you won't receive a review because your book is already "published." So go ahead and list your books—but hold off on actually shipping them until you've gotten your reviews. (It's probably somewhat safer to ship to wholesalers, because the reviewers are unlikely to ferret out your book in a bookstore; it's fairly easy for them, however, to do a quick online check on Amazon.)

- As long as you're mailing to a customer, be sure to take advantage of the opportunity: Stuff other literature—ads or flyers for your other books or products—into the mailing. (If you don't have other products of your own to offer, see if there are other vendors or publishers who have compatible products that you might offer—either in return for their offering your book, or for a percentage of the sales.)

- Always mail customers some "freebie" that they aren't expecting, to generate good will. (For example, everyone who orders a book in the **Publishing Game** series gets a complimentary list of "Hot Contacts" including contact information for wholesalers, chain stores, print and broadcast media movers and shakers, and more. (If you're reading this book at the library, send us a self-addressed, stamped envelope if you'd like this list and we'll pop one in the mail to you today.) Everyone who orders *all* our products—three books and several publishing kits—gets a complimentary gift.) Always, always offer something of value for free.

- Customers who order single books directly from you usually expect rapid delivery times of two to three days. This can only be achieved through FedEx® Express

Saver or 2nd Day Air, UPS 3 Day Select® or 2nd Day Air, or US Postal Service (USPS) Priority Mail. All offer free packaging for small orders. Priority Mail envelopes can be obtained free from any post office, or ordered for free from the USPS website, www.USPS.gov or by calling (800)222-1811. You can also order free envelopes directly from FedEx and UPS.

- Weigh your book and accompanying materials, including the envelope, and then see who offers the best prices. (Include the cost of the envelopes if the shipping company doesn't provide them for free.) Some companies charge by distance from the customer (number of "zones" crossed), some charge a flat rate for delivery within any part of the US. A flat rate is easier to explain to your customers. To be competitive, however, choose the cheapest shipping costs from one of the major shippers listed above; they are all reliable.

- Single books do not need to be shrink-wrapped to survive shipping in the stiff cardboard envelopes (such as USPS Priority Mail envelopes) but should be for shipping in soft envelopes like Tyvek (which, while strong, does not protect unwrapped books sufficiently.) All of the shipping companies mentioned above offer the stiff cardboard envelopes.

- Print shipping labels with your return address (and if you want to get fancy, your logo and possibly even a small ad). You can do this on your computer at home using any word-processing package and self-stick label stock made by any of a number of companies (e.g. Avery), available at office-supply stores nationwide.

- If you are only shipping a few books each day, you can just hand-address the mailing labels. Once your volume is more than 20-30 books per day, you'll probably want to have your shipping labels printed by your order-processing software (which, if your volume gets high enough, you will need). FedEx, UPS, and the US Postal Service all offer label-printing software, some of them available for free on-line; check out the web sites (www.uspswebtools.com/ShippingAssistant/, www.fedex.com, www.ups.com.).

- Similarly, for postage, once your volume exceeds 50-100 envelopes per day, you may want to consider a system that will print postage labels ("meter indicia") which you use instead of stamps. This adds a professional look to your mail, and may get you certain extra benefits (like free delivery confirmation.) There are several ways to go; here are your options:

  o Get a postage meter. According to US postal regulations, meters can only be rented, not purchased. Pitney-Bowes (www.pb.com) is the best known manufacturer of postage meters and related products. Office supply stores carry both postage meters and scales. After getting a meter at a local store, you will need to enter into a rental agreement with Pitney Bowes, and establish a Postage-by-Phone account. Then you can buy postage directly by telephone (it gets deposited into your postage meter through the telephone line.) You will be able to print any amount of postage on the meter that you want—first class, media mail, library rate, etc. (Weigh the envelope or package and check for the correct rate at the www.usps.com website.) All the information on purchasing postage is available at the Pitney-Bowes website.

o Another option is to use a so-called "PC postage" solution which provides software that lets you print postage (and address labels) from your home computer. You won't need a postage meter for this, just your inkjet or laser printer. Your postage can be printed on either envelopes or mailing labels easily; you can also integrate the software with your database, so you can download orders and print the postage automatically. These programs also calculate the postage rates for you and check addresses for errors. The cost is about $5 per month plus postage, with free trial periods. There are four companies currently authorized by the United States Postal Service (USPS) to do this:

- Neopost, Inc., 30955 Huntwood Avenue, Hayward, CA 94544-7084, 800-624-7892, www.neopostinc.com

- Pitney/Works, 1 Elmcroft Rd., Stamford, CT 06926-0700, www.pitneyworks.com

- Stamps.com, 3420 Ocean Park Boulevard Suite 1040, Santa Monica, CA 90405-3035, www.stamps.com

- Envelope Manager Software, 247 High Street, Palo Alto, CA 94301-1041, (800)576-3279 x140, www.endicia.com

- You can also use the USPS website itself to do this, `https://sss-web.usps.com/ds/jsps/index.jsp`

- Reliability: Our experience has been that fewer than 0.5% of our shipments fail to reach the customer (we use USPS Priority Mail for individual orders), so we don't bother with delivery confirmation or other shipping extras for individual orders. If a customer doesn't receive their order, we just ship them another one. If they fail to receive an order twice in a row (which has only happened to us once), then we do spring for the delivery confirmation.

- International orders can be handled the same way, except that you need to use one of the international shipping services offered by the same major shippers mentioned above. In addition to the USPS, FedEx, and UPS, there are other international package delivery companies to consider; for example, DHL (www.dhl.com). DHL claims to deliver to more areas of the world than any other company, and in fact, while traveling through the African bush, we did see DHL deliveries being made, and no evidence of any other shipping company anywhere. (On the other hand, how many books do you think you'll be sending to remote locations in the African bush?) The least expensive way to ship small quantities of books to certain countries (such as Australia) is with M bags through the postal service: Specify books/surface, and don't forget to double-box.

  o Be sure to attach a customs form (if shipping via USPS, use form CN22, available from any post office) to your international orders. Book orders you ship are considered "merchandise" on that form.

o Cost and delivery times for international orders differ, of course, dramatically from those for domestic orders (except for Canada, for which delivery times are close to that for domestic US shipments).

o Typical rates for air shipment by USPS Global Priority Mail are $9 for most countries, vs. $3.85 for domestic shipping. While it might be tempting to offer ground shipment of international orders (about $4 for many countries) for cost-sensitive customers, our experience is that the reliability of ground shipments is not as high, and the option is used by only a very small percentage of our international customers; we don't strongly recommend offering that option.

- Shipping bulk orders to wholesalers and distributors:

Wholesalers and distributors will order in larger quantities than individuals, commensurate with the success of your publicity initially, and longer term, with your actual sales (which, of course, depend on the success of your publicity). Once you get them ordering in multiples of the box-quantity for your book, your time spent packing orders will drop dramatically.

- You will need a variety of box sizes on hand. Initially, you will need boxes sized for a small number of books (1-10); later, you will need boxes sized to hold about half of the full-box-quantity of your book. Get one or two catalogs from office-supply stores, and determine which of their boxes will work for your books. Different stores offer somewhat different sizes of boxes. Office-supply stores have a variety of box-sizes available; there are also a large number of mail-order office-supply companies. A few good mail-order company for boxes are Uline (www.uline.com), BoxCity (www.BoxCity.com), Paper Mart (www.PaperMart.com), Tharco (www.Tharco.com), and Quill (www.Quill.com). Jesse Jones Box (www.JesseJonesBox.com) offers cardboard cases for boxed sets. If you can't get the correct size box for your book, invest in a box sizer (available at any office supply store.) With it, you can score the sides of the box, cut down the corners, and fold over the excess.

- Use strong, water-resistant clear tape; the cheapest of the clear acrylic box-sealing tapes is usually sufficient. These are available at office supply stores and by mail-order from one of the very many office supply stores on the web. Prices vary widely, and the mail-order places do not necessarily beat the bricks-and-mortar stores.

- Get packing material to cushion your books. Try to use something other than packing peanuts to pad out the box—everyone hates them because they get so messy. Instead, get a box of packing paper in a dispenser from U-Haul or BrownCor and wrap your book(s) neatly in packing paper. If you insist on peanuts, at least use the environmentally-friendly type, such as those made from wheat (or other vegetable) starch; one good product is the "UPSable Clean Green Loose Fill" available from BrownCor (www.browncor.com). High-volume shippers tend to prefer inflatable bags like those offered by Sealed Air (www.sealedair.com) or Novus (www.fpintl

.com), which weigh less (saving shipping costs), but these need specialized equipment to fill and seal the bags, usually beyond what starting publishers can justify.

- You should already have registered with FedEx and UPS as a shipper. You should have a roll of printed bar-code labels from them that you will attach to your packages to identify you. Get two kinds of labels: "Collect" labels, which you attach to boxes that someone else (your wholesaler or distributor) is paying to ship, and "Prepaid" labels, which you attach to boxes that you have to pay to ship. Along with the labels, you will also receive a log-book into which you write the addresses and shipping-label numbers of each box you ship. Be sure to use the right (collect vs. prepaid) label for each box.

- On your copy of the customer's purchase order, record the shipping ID's from the bar-code labels of each box that makes up that order, and of course, the date they were shipped, and the shipping company's name. Occasionally, you will receive a phone/fax/email message from your customer claiming they haven't received such-and-such an order; having dutifully recorded the shipping information, you can just look up the shipping numbers, and contact your shipper for a proof-of-delivery sheet, which you can then send to the customer. (The biggest wholesalers and chain stores are particularly prone to losing your shipments; keeping a careful shipment record means that you'll be able to prove that the error occurred at their end, rather than yours.)

- Books are reasonably sturdy, and do not need to be double-boxed (that is, they do not need to be placed in a box, which is then placed within another box), especially if you've shrink-wrapped the books in bundles (e.g. bundles of 5's). Make sure to use strong boxes (275 lb burst strength for boxes holding 30-40 pounds of books; less for lighter boxes), and sufficient padding material. Push the books into one corner of the box, and fill with peanuts all around the open two sides and the top; if you have room in the box, place the books in the middle and fill with peanuts around all 4 sides of the books, and the tops and bottoms. Seal the bottom of the box with 3 strips of tape (one down the middle along the seam of the flaps, and two on either side of that).

- Write the customer's purchase order number in a conspicuous place on your shipping label. Include the proper paperwork (usually at least a copy of their purchase order, and your invoice, if necessary) inside the box.

- Seal the top of the box with one strip of tape, then apply your shipping label and the shipping company's bar-code label, then add two more strips of tape across the box covering at least your shipping label. This helps protect the label from water, and ensures it will stay stuck on the box (self-stick labels sometimes come loose). Note, though, that certain types of labels printed with special label-printers are *not* supposed to be covered with tape, or the bar-codes on them won't be machine-readable.

- You're almost done! Call the shipping company to come pick up the boxes (there's usually a ~$10 charge per pickup, not per box, so if you get several orders each week, wait until you have a stack of boxes ready to go), or if convenient, drop the boxes off at one of the shipping company's box drop-off locations. Do not leave boxes outside an express pick-up box. You *may* be able to leave them at a third-party shipping center, such as a Mailboxes, Etc. store, but make sure that there isn't an extra charge for this. Usually, if you have a UPS or FedEx shipping label and have paid for the shipment or are shipping it collect you can drop your packages off at any authorized UPS or FedEx ground pick up location, including MailBoxes, Etc., for the standard rate rather than their [hefty!] UPS markup.)

Organize for Returns

One of the most frustrating norms of the publishing industry is the returns issue. Unless you have set non-returnable terms, which can be difficult to establish, all books are sold on consignment—to wholesalers, distributors, and bookstores—and are returnable at any point. Here are a few random things to keep in mind about returns:

- Consider selling your books non-returnable. You may find it harder to make sales initially, but at least books that are sold will stay sold.

- If you decide not to sell non-returnable, consider demanding that the wholesalers at least notify you before returning books. That way, you can prevent certain (disorganized) warehouses from returning and ordering books on the same day, at least.

- Do not automatically toss returned books into the garbage. Very often, wholesalers will return books because they are temporarily overstocked (due to poor planning) or because they've been the recipient of returned books. Depending on how they've been packaged, they might be in saleable condition. In this case, simply repackage them and send them out again.

- If the returned books are *not* in saleable condition, fill out the enclosed paperwork to return the shipment as an *unacceptable return.* Many small publishers don't bother doing this because of the time and paperwork hassle, but these returns can add up, and it is worth doing.

- When Ingram returns books that are coded with an OE (order entry) ending in XX, they will process your damage complaint. However, if it ends in XY, they will not accept return of the shipment, nor will they respond to inquiries. (Their explanation is that the XY indicates that the books were *received* damaged from the publisher.)

Day Number 29

Today you'll review and renew your **business plan** and **financial plan**.

Review and Renew Your Business and Financial Plans

Many publishers will question the need to do a business and financial plan in the first place. All the more so, they wonder, why bother reviewing the plans, now, at the end of a successful self-publishing project?

Now is *exactly* when you need to review your business and financial plans. Now, when the book production is finished, and you're about to plunge into the marketing phase of your book, spend an hour looking over your assumptions and numbers. Do you still think you'll sell as many books as you did a month ago? Did you incur different expenses than anticipated? Do you need to adjust your forecasts or your upcoming expenditures? Is the cash-flow working the way you anticipated? Write it all down—and keep these plans updated. If consulted on a monthly basis, they will prove your most valuable tools.

Day Number 30

Today you'll **plan for the next book!**

Plan for the Next Book

You're almost done! Now is the time to begin planning—for your *next* book.

- Run out quickly and buy the sequel to this book, **The Publishing Game: Bestseller in 30 Days** (or you can order it online at PublishingGame.com) so you can take your finished books and market them to bestsellerdom!

- When you go back for another printing of your book, be sure to include some of the reviews and quotations you've garnered on the back cover or in the front of the book. Remember to update the copyright page and change it to say "second printing."

- Start thinking now about the next book you're going to do. And try, *try* to write another book about the *same* topic. Aside from the fact that you can probably write your next book much more quickly (because you already know the issues) and can market it more effectively (because you know where to find the audience, and have developed an in-house list of buyers interested in that topic), you will also *sell more books*—because any customer, confronted in a bookstore with several books, two of whom are written *by the same person* will, all things being equal, buy one of those books—because the author looks

more authoritative, simply by virtue of the fact that she's
written two books on the same topic.

- One more idea for you: Once you have several books out
  on the same topic, you will have propelled yourself to
  that elusive "expert" status—and people will write to *you*,
  asking you to write blurbs for their books. Do it—it's the
  easiest way to get your name and book title out there!
  (And if they don't write to ask you—write to them with
  your quotation, anyway!) Spend some time to write a
  catchy, pithy, quotable quotation—so that you will be the
  one selected for the back cover and publicity material!

- Finally, if you will have several titles in the same niche,
  you can market them together (with perhaps a discount
  for readers who order the whole set) and you won't have
  to re-create the wheel each time you set out to market
  your new book.

- Throw a book party! You deserve it—and it's great for
  book sales. Invite everyone you know. Invite people you
  don't know who might be interested in your topic and
  pen a little note to them, so they know why they're being
  invited. Invite local press if you can provide a new idea
  or hot local angle. Most of all, invite family and friends
  and everyone who helped you get this book published.
  (Don't forget to invite me—I hate to miss a good party!)

This week you:

- **Did a final pre-print check**

- **Submitted your book to the printer**

- **Shipped your books from the printer**

- **Listed your book and publishing house**

- **Organized your shipping department**

- **Reviewed and renewed your business plan**

- **Planned for the next book**

Congratulations! If you've followed this plan, you should have a quality book that you've published yourself!

This concludes the 30-day plan to publish your book. (Next, order the sequel to this book, **The Publishing Game: Bestseller in 30 Days** to learn how to go from publisher to bestselling publisher! And follow up with **Expertizing** to learn how to be a name-brand in your field.)

If you've just been reading, but not following, the steps in this plan, now it's time to put down this book and *start publishing your own!* I wish you the best of luck.

Please write and let me know how it goes. Send me your thoughts, ideas, comments, corrections (and anything you wish I had included but didn't think of) to: PubComments@ PublishingGame.com.

Appendix A: Bibliography

Before you go home, there are a few other books and resources you should know about. There are a quazillion books on the market about self publishing and self-promotion, and I'm only recommending here the ones I personally found particularly useful. There are many others, and many that are not yet on the market. Read as many as you can get your hands on. Even a book that offers one interesting tip or one new idea is worth the time you've spent on it. All it takes is one brilliant new idea to make a bestseller.

If you like the day-by-day organization of this book, try my sequel, **The Publishing Game: Bestseller in 30 Days**, for a complete 30-day plan that explains how to go from unknown to bestseller! Then read my book, **Expertizing** to learn how to become a name-brand in your field and how to be quoted in national newspapers and magazines.

On the other hand, if you've decided after reading this that publishing is way too much work, and you'd rather just write your books and let someone else sell them, try reading **The Publishing Game: Find an Agent in 30 Days**. (Just so you know—I did—four times.)

If there's a child in your life who is interested in following in your footsteps, be sure to pick up a copy of my **Kids**

Publish! If there's a corporate type in your life, steer her towards **Consultants Publish**.

John Kremer's *1001 Ways to Market Your Book* is truly a book marketing Bible. Buy it.

Dan Poynter's *The Self-Publishing Manual* has successfully launched more self-publishers than any other book. Likewise, Marilyn and Tom Ross's *The Complete Guide to Self-Publishing* offers a wealth of useful publishing information.

Every independent publisher should read at least one or two books on book design. My favorites are Robin Williams' *The Non-Designer's Design Book* and Roger C. Parker's *One-Minute Designer.*

To learn more about the printing process, you might want to take a look at Helmut Kipphan's *Handbook of Print Media.* At the very least, check out the International Paper Information's *Pocket Pal.*

Suzanne P. Thomas's *Make Money Self-Publishing* offers profiles of several small publishers and how they are succeeding. The book is both inspiring and educational.

To enroll in a gritty, information-packed one-day workshop with Fern Reiss on how to self-publish your book, how to make your book a bestseller, and how to find a literary agent see the workshop schedule at **PublishingGame.com**.

Appendix B: Budget

This is a sample budget, based on expenses for my recent book, "Terrorism and Kids: Comforting Your Child," (www.TerrorismAndKids.com).

Keep in mind that I didn't have certain expenses (I already had basic office equipment and my publishing house was already set up); that I chose to do certain tasks rather than pay someone else to do them (answering my own telephone calls, order fulfillment); that I spend very little on advertising and not much more on publicity services (because I don't believe in spending much money on these items); and that my favorite expenditure is joining associations and attending conferences (but I'm currently marketing seven books, so that cost, though listed below in its entirety, should really be amortized.)

Also keep in mind that I made certain decisions based on the nature of this book (that I needed to spend more to rush it into print quickly, incurring additional cover design expenses, for example) and on my understanding of the publishing industry (that I wouldn't sell these books returnable—which meant that fewer books were sold, since some libraries and bookstores won't buy books except on consignment, but that I didn't have to worry about any of the "sold" books coming back six months later.)

You don't need to spend exactly where I spent—and shouldn't, since every book, and every situation, is different—but this will give you an idea of the sorts of budgetary decisions that need to be made, and the sorts of tradeoffs you can consider.

- Interior book design: Free—did it myself. I didn't have the luxury of time to fence this out to someone else to do. If you have the time, or don't have a good eye, this might be worth spending money on.

- Cover art: $2500. (Probably somewhat more than you will need to spend; this was a rush job as I went to press on September 19th to serve the 9/11 market.)

- Printing: As of March, 2002, I had printed 7,500 copies of the book, at a total cost of $12,000. This included the cost to matte laminate the cover of the books (I wouldn't do this with most books, but it looked right for this title) and to shrink-wrap in bundles of five (I find fewer books are damaged in storage and shipping if I shrink-wrap.)

- Shipping: Free. I happened to use a local printer and drove the books home in a minivan each print run. And all of my shipments to wholesalers are paid for by the wholesaler, because that is one of the terms I set. If you go with a standard contract you'll pay for that shipping (and the returns) and if you use a non-local printer, your shipping costs might run several hundred dollars per print run. Be sure to mention your organization memberships to get their shipping discounts.

- Galleys: $10. I sent only five galleys for this book, because I printed books one week after my manuscript was completed. Rather than go to the time and expense of having five galleys produced, I ripped covers off five finished books, and had them bound in cardboard at Kinko's. The cost of galleys can run as much as $15-20 per galley, and ordinarily you might need anywhere from ten to a hundred.

- Memberships: $500. I am a member of PMA, SPAN, the American Booksellers Association, and several regional bookseller organizations. (I like organizations.)

- Contests: $200. I entered this book in PMA's Benjamin Franklin Awards for $60; Foreword Magazine's contest for $50; Independent Publishers contest for $60 and Parents' Choice award for $50.

- Book Displays: $260. I paid PMA to have the book displayed at Book Expo America, the Public Library Association show, and the Frankfurt Book Fair. I also displayed at several regional library association meetings, and several educational and psychological conferences.

- Postage: $700. I do spend a lot on postage, but this also included the postage costs for several other books, so it's hard to say how much of this I would have incurred just on this title.

- Postcards and associated mailings: $2500. This turned into one of my biggest ticket items for this book, since because of the timing, I paid other companies to do my mailings; often I label, stamp, and mail them myself. The postcards themselves usually cost only around $350 or $400 for 5,000 postcards total; the cost of the mailings (I did one mailing through one of the postcard places, and had Sam Decalo of Florida Academic Press do the others) accounts for the remainder. The postcard was mailed to hundreds of independent publishers and libraries, generating book sales that are ongoing.

- Publicity: $1100. I spent about $150 buying media lists from Kate Bandos' a la carte publicity service; I spent $250 on Paul Krupin's fax service to over 1000 journalists; I spent $200 getting a subscription to PartyLine and another $500 on a subscription to Dan Janal's PR Leads. As you can guess, I prefer a la carte publicity services, because I can control the money and get exactly the services I want. I also spent considerably more on this book than I usually do on publicity, because I was afraid the topical nature of the material would render the book obsolete before I could recoup my expenses if I didn't spend some more up front to move it faster. In retrospect, I wish I'd spent even more, especially earlier, and gotten the word out that much faster. But that decision varies from book to book.

- Conferences: $700. I attended PMA's Publishing University in New York, but since I was giving one of the talks, my conference tuition was waived, as was my entrance fee to Book Expo America. My total costs in NY (including accommodations and food) were about $700 (for the whole family). I made contact with dozens of movers and shakers in the publishing industry, and sold the rights to **The Publishing Game: Bestseller in 30 Days** to Writer's Digest Book Club while I was there, so I consider it money well spent. (Unfortunately my three children, who spent a delightful few days acquiring free stuffed animals, novelty items, and wonderful books at Book Expo America, now want to go every year, which was not part of my planned budget!)

How did the book do? Well, I got reviews in American Library Association's BookList Magazine, Foreword Magazine, and several mentions in Publishers Weekly; I received quotes from notables including Senator Edward Kennedy; and the book received a 2002 American Booksellers Association BookSense selection and was nominated for a Parents Choice Award.

I sold 7,000 books in six months, and currently have a (large) quantity sale pending. My total gross income on each book was $6.72 on the ones I sold through wholesalers (many of them); on my non-wholesale sales my gross per book was much higher. My total gross was well over $50,000. Accounting for my expenses, and not including taxes (and remember, these figures are slightly misleading because several of my expenses should have been amortized over all the books I am currently marketing), I netted approximately $30,000 in six months.

Just as a comparison: *The Infertility Diet: Get Pregnant and Prevent Miscarriage* on which I worked approximately five hours per week for the past three years (it's definitely a backlist title), has sold over 12,000 books at $24.95 each (net $11.23 per book from wholesalers), grossing over $100,000 during that time. It, too, continues to sell steadily.

You do the math.

Index

A

ABA. *See* Book Buyers
  Handbook
ABI, 79, 80, 164
Academic Book Center,
  111
Acumen. *See* Software,
  Financial
Advance Review Copies.
  See Galleys
Alt-Publish, 131
Amazon.com, 218
American Society of
  Indexers, 192
Anderson, Eric, 91
Anserphone, 120
Answering Service
  Professionals, 120
ARCs. *See* Galleys

B

Back Matter, 190
Baker & Taylor, 111
Bank Accounts, 72

Barcodes, 135
Barnes and Noble, 166
BarnesAndNoble.com,
  219
Bell, Pat, 132
Berkeley, Susan, 119
Biblio, 104
BISAC, 140
Book Buyers Handbook,
  84, 86
Book Clearing House, 116,
  121
Book House, The, 110
Book Listings, Fixing, 216
Booklist, 161, 162
BookMasters, 116
BookPeople, 109
Books in Print, 31
Books-A-Million, 167, 220
Bookstores
  online, 113
Bookstores, online, 218
BookZone, 91, 132
Borders, 167
Bowker, R.R., 75
Bowker, RR, 77
Boxes, 226

Brodart, 110
Budget
    sample, 239
Bullen, Martha. *See* Cover
    Text
Business Plan, 43, 232

C

Cash-Flow Statement, 47
Cataloging in Publication.
    See CIP
Cat's Pajamas. *See*
    Software, Financial
Chain Stores, 164
Chapters, 167
Choice, 218
CIP, 168, 169, 170, 217
Clipper Express, 213
Consortium, 104
Copyright Page, 186
Copyrights, 139, 173
    permission, 67
Cover Design, 142, 144
Cover Text, 33, 35
    writing, 140
Cox, Jim, 132, 218
Credit Cards. *See* Merchant
    Account
Culleton, John, 218

D

Dewey, 169
Digital Drone Studios, 91
Distributors, 103, 109
    bankruptcy, 105
    exclusive, 103, 104
    non-exclusive, 108
    PMA program, 105
Donnelley, RR, 97

E

Editing, 150
Email Newsletter Kit. *See*
    Special Reports
Emery Pratt, 110

F

Fax. *See* Telephone Line
Fearless Book Reviews,
    218
Feldman, Diane, 152
Financial Plan, 47
Foreword Magazine, 162
Freight Management
    Systems, 213
Front Matter, 185
Fulfillment Houses, 114
Future Thru Group, 91

G

Galleys, 153, 155, 164
  Amazon warning, 160
Goldinger, Sharon, 151

H

Harnish, John, 102
Hayskar, Bonnie, 113
Hoffman, Ivan, 68
Horowitz, Shel. *See* Cover
  Text

I

Independent Bookstore
  Publicity Kit. *See* Special
  Reports
Independent Publishers
  Group, 104, 105
Indexing, 191
Index-L, 192
IndyBook, 113
Ingram, 85, 111
Ingram Sales Line, 25
Insurance. *See* Liability
  Insurance
Intrepid Group, 115
ISBN, 75, 78, 135

J

Jassin, Lloyd, 69

K

Kahn, Laurie, 152
Katz & Mouse, 91
Kerrigan, Barry, 142, 176
Kids Publish, 237
Kirkus Reviews, 162
Kirsch, Jonathan, 68
Kremer, John, 141, 238

L

Layout, 176
LC, 169
Leardi, Jeanette, 152
Legal Structure, 62
Liability Insurance, 69
Library Journal, 161
Library of Congress, 168,
  173
Lightbourne, 143
Literary Agents Kit. *See*
  Special Reports
Literary Market Place, 216
Long, Mayapriya, 142, 176

M

MARC, 168

Market Research. *See*
    Ingram Sales Line
    action list, 29
Masterson, Pete, 132, 142,
    176
Merchant Account, 122
Microsoft Money. *See*
    Software, Financial
Midpoint, 105
Midwest Book Review,
    132, 218
Midwest Library Service,
    110
Mountain West, 120
Myrlyn. *See* Software,
    Financial

N

NAIPR, 111
National Book Network,
    105
Networks, support, 130
New Leaf, 109
New York Times Book
    Review, 162

P

Partners Book
    Distributing, 104
PatLive, 119
PCN, 168, 169

Peachtree. *See* Software,
    Financial
Plan. *See* Financial Plan,
    See Business Plan
POD, 94
Post Office Box, 72
Postage Meters, 223
Poynter, Dan, 238
PPI, 144, 201, 210
Price
    setting the, 35
Print on Demand. *See*
    POD
Printers, 194, 199, 210
Profit and Loss Statement,
    47
Progress Chart, 127
Pub 123. *See* Software,
    Financial
Pub-forum, 131
Pub-L, 131
Publication Date
    choosing a, 41
Publishers Assistant. *See*
    Software, Financial
Publishers Group West,
    104
Publishers Marketing
    Association, 130
    meet the buyers day, 165
Publishers Weekly, 160,
    161
Publishing House

choosing a name, 56
establishing your, 72

Q

Quality Books, 172
Quebecor, 97
Quickbooks. *See* Software,
    Financial
Quicken. *See* Software,
    Financial

R

Rayve Productions, 115
Requests for Quotation,
    199
Returns. *See* Terms
Reviews, 233
    Booklist, 162
    Fearless Book Reviews,
        218
    Foreword Magazine, 162
    Kirkus Reviews, 162
    Library Journal, 161
    Midwest Book Review,
        218
    Publishers Weekly, 161
RFQs, 199
Rich, Lloyd, 68
Ross, Marilyn and Tom,
    238
Rowse Reviews, 218

S

SAN, 78
Sansevieri, Penny, 102
School Library Journal,
    163
SCORE, 133
Sell Your Book to
    Corporations Kit. *See*
    Special Reports
Shipping, 213, 220
Shopping Carts, 124
Small Business
    Administration, 133
Software. *See Shopping Carts*
Software, SSL, 125
SPAN, 131
Special Reports
    Email Newsletter Kit, 256
    Independent Bookstore
        Publicity Kit, 256
    Literary Agents Kit, 256
    Sell Your Books to
        Corporations Kit, 256
    Special Reports Kit, 256
    Syndicate Yourself Kit,
        256
    Top Amazon Reviewers,
        256
Special Reports Kit. *See*
    Special Reports
Spine Width, 144, 201, 210
SSL. *See* Software, SSL
STOP. *See* Terms

Syndicate Yourself Kit. *See* Special Reports

T

Telephone Line, 73, *See* answering services, 119
toll-free, 117
Terms, 81, 82
discount, 81, 82
returns, 82
STOP, 80, 83
Terry, Pamela, 142, 176
The Publishing Game
Find an Agent in 30 Days, 237
The Publishing Game: Publish a Book in 30 Days, 237
Thomas, Suzanne P., 238
Title
choosing a, 23, 29
planning future, 84
Title Page, 185
Top Amazon Reviewers. *See* Special Reports
Trademarks, 32, 69
TX. *See* Copyrights

U

UCC, 107
UPC, 79, 138

W

Website
Author's Guild, 91
establish a, 87
listing your, 92
order taking, 121
Website Domain Names, 31
Wholesalers, 103, 109, 111
library, 110
Writers Collective, 102

Y

Yellow Transportation, 214

Z

Zerner, Larry, 68

About the Author

Fern Reiss is an honors graduate from Harvard University. She writes frequently for magazines including Sesame Street, Parent & Child, Moment, and Parade. She is the award-winning author of *Terrorism and Kids: Comforting Your Child*, *The Infertility Diet: Get Pregnant and Prevent Miscarriage*, *The Publishing Game: Bestseller in 30 Days*, *The Publishing Game: Find an Agent in 30 Days*, *Kids Publish!*, *Consultants Publish*, and *Expertizing*.

Fern consults with aspiring authors on traditional publishing, self-publishing, and how to be quoted in the major media. She speaks nationally at writing and publishing conferences including Publishers Marketing Association University, the NY and Los Angeles Learning Annexes, the New England Council of Child and Adolescent Psychiatry, and the NY Small Press Center. More information on her books, consulting, and speaking, including an up-to-date list of her intensive one-day publishing workshops, can be found at www.PublishingGame.com.

Publishing Game Workshops

If you enjoyed this book, and would like to learn more about publishing and marketing your own book, consider one of Fern Reiss's Publishing Game workshops.

For a fraction of the cost of a private consultation, you can benefit from a full-day of Fern's top-notch advice and guidance, in a collegial setting of fellow writers and publishers. Fern's one-day workshops are $195—and will save you from making many thousands of dollars of mistakes. (Also they're great fun!)

You'll get hundreds of tips on finding literary agents, marketing and promoting, getting into and working with the chain stores, and pursuing special sales. Get the latest, most up-to-date publishing information that will help make your next project a publishing success.

Workshops are planned for Boston, New York, New Jersey, Connecticut, Boca Raton, Seattle, Los Angeles, San Francisco, Chicago, Philadelphia, and Washington DC.

More dates and locations are coming soon. If you don't see your city on our list, find five friends who would like to attend and call us with your request! We'd be happy to schedule additional workshops as time and scheduling permit.

You can email us for more information at PubWorkshops@ PublishingGame.com or you can register online at PublishingGame.com.

Publishing Game Order Form

Yes, I want to create a bestseller... Send me:

__The Publishing Game: Bestseller in 30 Days $19.95
__The Publishing Game: Publish a Book in 30 Days $19.95
__The Publishing Game: Find an Agent in 30 Days $19.95
__Kids Publish! $18.95
__Consultants Publish $19.95
__Expertizing $19.95

__**Literary Agents Kit**, $49—This Special Report details includes information & emails for over 100 top literary agents.

__**Sell Your Books to Corporations Kit**, $49—Sell to Fortune 100 corporations. Letters, contracts, addresses (no emails).

__**Top Amazon Reviewers**, $49—Contact information (some addresses, some emails) for many top Amazon reviewers.

__**Independent Bookstore Publicity Kit**, $49—Contact independent bookstores directly! Includes emails and details.

__**Email Newsletter Kit** $49—Learn the fastest and best way to launch your own email newsletter. All the details you'll need.

__**Syndicate Yourself Kit** $49—Everything you need to know to syndicate your writing to newspapers nationwide!

__**Special Reports Kit** $49—All the details you need to know to learn how to sell special reports quickly and easily.

__**The whole enchilada!**—All seven special reports for $300.

Enclose $4 for priority mail ($10 outside the U.S.) & mail, or fax your name, address, zip, telephone, email, and credit card including expiration date to:

Peanut Butter and Jelly Press, LLC
P.O. Box 590239, Newton, MA 02459-0002
(617)630-0945 phone/fax, orders@PublishingGame.com

Sign up a one-day intensive publishing workshop with author Fern Reiss! See PublishingGame.com for details.